CHAPTERS

with its wonderful Edwardian interiors, the Nag's Head opposite the stage door of the Opera House, with its collection of photographs, The Lamb and Flag in Rose Court, with the Dryden Room upstairs, the Sheffield in Long Acre and the Nell Gwynn in Drury Lane, to name just a few. Each pub has its own unique history.

7. ***Special Places***. ....The Crush Bar at The Royal Opera House, The Garrick Club, the Actor's Church, the like of which are not found anywhere else in England.

8. ***Covent Garden Ghosts.*** ....Take a theatre tour backstage to find your own, or down a side street at night. This book tells you where to find them.

9. ***Interesting Hotels***. ....Notorious, luxurious, historic, all fabulous places to stay. From the Waldorf and Number One in the Aldwych, to the Mountbatten and The .....Covent Garden Hotel near Seven Dials, converted from the French Hospital, to the Fieldings in Broad Court, The St. Martins, a recent addition to St. Martin's Lane

10. ***Covent Garden Walk***. ....Visit the places described in this book with details of why these places are unique and unforgetable.

POSTSCRIPT...Living and working in Covent Garden

London's Notorious Covent Garden Revisited

The Cultural Heart of London

Rules Restaurant

The Lamb and Flag

The Ivy

Goodwin's Court

St. Paul's Church

Clos Maggiore Restaurant

The True Story of Covent Garden

ELIZABETH SHARLAND

LONDON'S NOTORIOUS COVENT GARDEN REVISITED
The Cultural Heart of London

On the cover: Steve Ross with author celebrating the songs of Covent Garden.

iUniverse books may be ordered through booksellers or by contacting:

iUniverse
1663 Liberty Drive
Bloomington, IN 47403
www.iuniverse.com
1-800-Authors (1-800-288-4677)

ISBN: 978-1-5320-7333-5 (hc)
ISBN: 978-1-5320-7334-2 (sc)
ISBN: 978-1-5320-7335-9 (e)

Library of Congress Control Number: 2019904594

Print information available on the last page.

iUniverse rev. date: 04/24/2019

London's Notorious Covent Garden Revisited

The Cultural Heart of London
Discover its cultural heart and notorious history…..Past and Present.
By Elizabeth Sharland

Acknowledgements:
Paul Ibell, John Gander, Colman Jones, Jane Gussin.

Every effort has been made to trace all copyright holders, but if any have been inadvertently been overlooked, the author and publishers will be pleased to make the necessary arrangements at the first opportunity.

Dedicated to Joe Sirola

Other Books by Elizabeth Sharland

Passionate Pilgrimages..from Chopin to Coward.
Love From Shakespeare to Coward
From Shakespeare to Coward
The British on Broadway
A Theatrical Feast of London
A Theatrical Feast of New York
A Theatrical Feast of Paris
The Best Actress (Novel)
Blue Harbour Revisited…a Gift from Noel Coward (Novel)
On the Riviera...a Novel
Classical Destinations
The British Invasion of Broadway Continues
www.sharland.com

Author's Note.

This book was written as a record of various historic buildings and beautiful places in Covent Garden because in 50 years time, most of them will have disappeared. The first edition was written in 2009, and now ten years later you will see just how many places even after such a short time have disappeared already.

Fortunately Rules Restaurant, the oldest restaurant in London, still remains as one of the highlights of this fascinating area.

Contents

Preface

People who read about Covent Garden have widely different interests. Some are historians, some are performers and some may be visiting the area for the first time. The hidden history covers many centuries and unusual celebrities, from Nell Gywnn, King Charles's mistress to Princess Diana, dancing for Prince Charles onstage at the Royal Opera House. Royalty has spent time here and the Royal Opera House has its own Royal Box. World famous opera and ballet stars appear here in front of Kings and Queens. Princess Margaret was once the Patron and now it is Prince Charles.

The streets have had buskers and street performers for centuries and they can still be seen there today as well as serious classical musicians who play in the Piazza.

Obviously creative talent is aroused by emotional and intellectual stimulus, physically and mentally. Many would agree that some of these creative people have dysfunctional or more unusual, or more unnatural desires than others. Therefore the more shocking details often found in biographies often points the way to their creativity. It has been written that people who have unhappy childhoods want to become actors, and that writers drink, because it releases great ideas and creativity. All kinds can be found in Covent Garden and I find it an absolutely unique area, with so many characters both alive and dead who play their parts on this wonderful stage.

It would be interesting to read about the latest fashionable shops, popular pubs and hotels that existed in Covent Garden a 100 years ago but there is no accurate record as far as I know.

This book, therefore, maybe of interest in 100 years hence when we are all gone. There are biographies of the people who lived and worked here of course, and some of the restaurants and theatres they visited are still in existence, but in 100 years time, they maybe all gone too.

While doing research for this book I came across the writings of theatre people, who had lived and worked in Covent Garden, when I was a student, and who had inspired me although they were a little before my time. They have a chapter in this book. Clemence Dane, (Winifred Ashton) Alan Dent, Angus McBean, James Agate all wrote about the area and their stories make fascinating reading.

CHAPTER ONE

People – Highwaymen and Harlots

Who lives in Covent Garden? The answer depends on the century in question, as the area has changed so much down the years.

When Covent Garden (as we know it today) was first developed, under the auspices of Inigo Jones, it was designed as a luxurious residential area, with the central Piazza surrounded by grand houses. The aristocracy were already familiar with the area, for the ground between the present-day Strand (Covent Garden's southern boundary) and the Thames was a traditional site for mansions, lining the route between the City of London and the Court at Whitehall.

So in these early days, the local residents were the wealthy, lured by the latest architecture and domestic technology into a new, healthy development that was convenient for both commerce and access to the King.

After the Civil War, the execution of King Charles I (1649) and the brief Republic, Charles II's restoration saw the return of the monarchy – and of the theatre. When the King returned, so did the theatre, focussed on the Theatre Royal, Drury Lane. He began an affair with an actress, Nell Gwynn who is still remembered today and had two pubs named after her.

Along with the theatres came the fruit and vegetable market, whose location in the heart of the residential area inevitably reduced its appeal for many householders, who found the noise and crowds that went with a bustling market, intolerable. At the same time, the area we now know as St James's was being developed, by Henry Jermyn (later Earl of St Albans) who was the lover of the Queen Mother, Henrietta Maria, after whom Henrietta Street (to the west of the Piazza) is named.

St James's blossomed in the later 17th century while districts like Bloomsbury were developed in the 18th century, and in the course of this the smart money and society families moved with the times, leaving Covent Garden to a lower level of social class, one which reflected the theatrical profession, which was not, in those days, considered a calling for a true gentleman.

A by-product of this was that as the society matrons moved out, the brothel madams moved in, and Covent Garden became notorious for its prostitutes – of both sexes. Plying one's trade outside the theatres and in the little alleyways that criss-crossed the whole area (many of which still survive today, like little architectural time capsules) was a profitable if dangerous trade, not least because of the prevalence of sexually transmitted diseases and the lack of reliable and safe cures.

Sexual morality in general was far freer in Covent Garden than anywhere else in London, free as it was from the long-established authorities in the City. Among those who chose to live in the area were the notorious highwayman Jack Shepherd. Jack was a slim young man with an amazing talent for escaping from prison. Had he been more talented as a thief he would have had les need for such daring break-outs but as it was he was based at the White Hart Inn (now demolished, near the Aldwych) and it was from here that he was on more than one occasion arrested. He even managed to escape from Newgate, one of London's most notorious gaols, but was eventually executed at Tyburn.

The site of Tyburn, where the capital's principal gallows was located, is at today's Marble Arch, and the route was along today's High Holborn and Oxford Street, to the north of Covent Garden.

Jack failed to escape from the cart that trundled from the City to Tyburn, but the plan was for his friends to grab his body. Criminals were in those days hanged slowly rather than having their necks broken by a sudden drop, so if they were taken down when supposedly dead, they could sometimes be revived, out of sight of the authorities, and thereby escape their coffin to start all over again.

Unfortunately young Jack Shepherd's plan was foiled by his very popularity. When his friends claimed his body, the crowd of spectators thought these men were surgeons who wanted to dissect the corpse (the only way doctors could legally study anatomy) so they tried to stop them. In the course of the brief but violent struggle, Jack's body – whether alive or just nearly dead – was so badly battered that his friends were unable to revive him. He was buried in St Martin's in the Fields, the church at the very furthest south-western corner of Covent Garden, on the edge of Trafalgar Square.

If Jack Shepherd was a loveable rogue, then Nell Gwynn was an adorable actress. Starting as a teenager, she quickly graduated from selling oranges (and, allegedly, her body) to acting on stage and becoming the mistress of King Charles II. Samuel Pepys was one of the actress's many fans, though he had to be content with watching her on stage. She was far too ambitious to let such a serial womaniser anywhere near her, and her ambition, persistence and natural charms eventually got her the first prize in Restoration London – the King's bed.

Charles had a number of mistresses, often with several on the go at the same time, but Nell was always one of his favourites, and was easily the most popular with the locals. When Charles was dying he asked "Let not poor Nelly starve" but it was TB that got her in the end, not poverty, and all the fine clothes and full coffers that her public career and private charms had earned her were no use against the Grim Reaper.

Another actress associated with the area, but two centuries later, was Lily Langtry, the so-called 'Jersey Lily', who was the mistress of another highly-sexed English monarch, Edward VII. As Prince of Wales he courted Lily in the private dining room sof Rules, located above the ground floor public area. Edward was not the only famous man to be smitten with La Langtry – her friend Oscar Wilde also swooned over her, though in a less carnal fashion that His Royal Highness.

The private dining rooms at Rules were, thanks to Edward, given a very racy reputation, which only added to their popularity. Restauranteurs, as well as newspaper editors, have always been very aware that sex sells.

Writing racy reports about famous people can backfire, however, as the poet and playwright Dryden found when he was badly beaten up outside the Lamb and Flag Pub (see the chapter on pubs and wine bars) as a result of the Earl of Rochester's fury at a satire making fun of the aristocrat's love life.

The playwright and theatre owner Richard Brinsley Sheridan had to fight two duels to preserve the honour of his wife, Elizabeth Linley, from a would-be suitor who refused to take no for an answer from the beautiful singer. A duel was also fought by the actor Charles Macklin, who is rumoured to have killed another actor in a swordfight. Thespians live on heightened emotion, off-stage as well as on, which may be why so many of them seem to have taken to the sword to settle disputes.

Today you will find that the people who live here are mostly connected with the Arts including the culinary ones. There are many theatres as well as restaurants, so the area is filled with actors, singers, dancers, writers, artists and chefs. Many of them live here often in tiny studios and flats. Their day starts early in the morning and ends late at night.

Sir Thomas Beecham, once Artistic Director at the Royal Opera House, was asked why he chose such generously-proportioned leading ladies for the soprano roles, rejecting the more attractive candidates, the director replied, "Those sopranos who sing like birds, eat like horses, and vice versa."

When Charles Dickens moved into Tavistock House, he made sure that every detail of it was to his taste. One of the features he installed was a hidden door to his study, made to look like part of an unbroken wall of books, complete with dummy shelves and fictitious titles. Dickens clearly derived much amusement from the invention of titles for these volumes. They ranged from the purely facetious—*Five Minutes in China,* three volumes, and *Heaviside's Conversations with Nobody*—to straight puns, such as *The Gunpowder Magazine.* In later years he added *Cat's Lives* (nine volumes) and *The Wisdom of Our Ancestors,* which consisted of volumes on ignorance, superstition, the block, the stake, the rack, dirt, and disease. The companion—*The Virtues of Our Ancestors*—was so narrow the title had to be printed sideways.

Covent Garden Market

CHAPTER TWO

COVENT GARDEN'S THEATRES

As the historic heart of London's theatre district, Covent Garden has the highest concentration of theatre buildings in the capital. It has two opera houses: The Royal Opera House, Covent Garden, to give it its full title, and the London Coliseum. The Royal Opera House is home to the Royal Ballet and the Royal Opera, while the Coliseum is the base of English National Opera but also hosts regular dance seasons by visiting companies, principally English National Ballet.

The Royal Opera house suddenly became very popular with the masses, after the Three Tenors became famous and everybody wanted to see and hear them sing, even though they appeared solo at Covent Garden in different operas. It has been the scene of tumultous applause, overnight successes, huge fame for opera and ballet stars, as well as the unforgetable farewell appearances of divas and dancers including Dame Joan Sutherland and Dame Margot Fonteyn.

The theatres that can be found within Covent Garden's borders are The Adelphi, The Vaudeville, The Aldwych, the Novello, The Duchess, The Lyceum, The Theatre Royal, Drury Lane, The Donmar, The Fortune – and the little Tristan Bates Theatre, which is part of the Actor's Centre and which was named after the teenage son of actor Sir Alan Bates. Tristan died in Japan, and his mother, Victoria, died not long after, it is said of a broken heart. Unlike the other theatres, it is a very modern construction and is often used for avant garde plays.

Alan Bates was not only a great stage actor he was also a movie star and a leading man on television, too. His death, of cancer, in 2003 was a great loss, not just to the London stage, but to that of New York: his last great stage success was on Broadway, in Fortune's Fool, for which he got a Tony. He appeared, in this and other plays, with his surviving twin son, Benedict.

Of the major theatres listed above, the one most similar in size (though far more traditional in design) is the Fortune Theatre. This is a rare example of 1920s theatre architecture in central London, and opened with a play called Sinners. What the congregation of the Church (which partially shares the site with the theatre) made of this can only be imagined. Let's hope they had a sense of humour.

One group who certainly had this was the Cambridge Footlights, the group of young Cambridge students who took their revues from the gilded domes of academe to the West End in the early 60s, when their series of sketches, called Beyond the Fringe, was performed at the Fortune Theatre and helped make the fortunes of a number of its cast, including Dudley Moore, Peter Cook, Jonathan Miller and Alan Bennett.

The Fortune sits at the side of the vast structure of The Theatre Royal, Drury Lane. The first theatre on this site was established in 1663, three years after the return of the monarchy (under King Charles II, elder son of the beheaded Charles I.) Charles restored not just the crown but the theatre, which had been banned by Cromwell and his Puritan cohorts. There had never been any love lost between George III and his heir ; indeed his legendary dislike of his eldest son accounts for the extraordinary fact of there being two royal boxes at Drury Lane.

The incident that sparked this was that when the King came across the Prince of Wales in the foyer of the theatre, in a fit of rage he physically attacked him ! The King was eventually restrained, but it was decided that, in order to prevent such an unseemly event occurring again, there should be two royal boxes, each with their own staircase --- hence the King's Side and the Prince's Side today. Once in their boxes, though they could not avoid seeing each other, they were at least prevented from coming to blows.

There was nothing to stop other people from having a go at them, however. Boxes were designed for the occupants to be seen, rather than for them to see the stage, which is why the sight lines from them are generally bad (in all theatres), and why today's Royals often prefer to be seated in the middle of the Dress Circle, rather than in a box.

George III was on one such visit to Drury Lane, accompanied by Sheridan, when a madman attempted to assassinate him with a pistol shot. Fortunately his aim was as poor as his reasoning, and the King was able to wave to a relieved audience. Sheridan, quick-witted as ever, composed an impromptu extra verse to the National Anthem (about saving the King from assassins) and had the orchestra play it to a delighted King and his enthusiastic subjects.

Drury Lane – the current playhouse is the fourth on the site - has seen it all, and has the ghosts to prove it, as discussed in chapter XX. It has not surprisingly been best known, for over a century, for musicals. It has a vast stage with amazing stage technology, which was removed for the run of The Lord of the Rings and has since been put back in place, under the benign supervision of English Heritage.

Among the musicals have been Noel Coward's Pacific 1860, (a rare flop for The Master) and of course Ivor Novello's massive 1930s hits, which collectively established him as a leading figure in British musical theatre and also helped save Drury Lane from potential closure – something which seems inconceivable now, but which was very much on the cards in 1934. Novello's shows were Glamorous Night (1935), Careless Rapture (1936), Crest of the Wave (1937) and The Dancing Years (1939).

More modern hits have included Miss Saigon (the theatre's longest-running musical) and The Producers. The latter show opened at Drury Lane after having wowed audiences at the St James's in New York, and one of the leads from the original production, Nathan Lane, came over to London, where he played opposite British comedian and actor Lee Evans.

The theatre has a beautiful interior and public rooms, with a sweeping staircase and a fabulous main bar, the Grand Saloon, which hosts many regular theatre events, from book prizes to the Baddeley Cake ceremony, where the resident company celebrates Twelfth Night with cakes and punch – the cake's decoration always reflecting the show currently running at the theatre.

Another musical that was premiered in New York but moved equally successfully to London was My Fair Lady, which was staged here in the 1950s. The portico of St Paul's Church, Covent Garden, where Eliza first meets Henry Higgins, is only a few minutes walk away from the equally imposing portico of the Theatre Royal.

Closer to the theatre (indeed, almost opposite it) is the little Duchess Theatre. This tends to present small-scale plays, including one-man shows. Most recently (at the time of writing) it staged Plague over England. About the anti-gay atmosphere of 1950s London, it focuses on the arrest and brief trial of the great classical actor, Sir John Gielgud, who was found guilty of a sexual misdemeanour (with a consenting male adult) in 1953.

The play was written by the theatre critic of London's major evening paper, The Evening Standard. So enthusiastic were the reviews of his fellow critics that he decided to give up his job and concentrate of playwriting full time!

Other shows at the Duchess have included a scaled-down version of the hit musical, Buddy, about the tragically short life and remarkable career of Buddy Holly. Maureen Lipman, a great favourite with West End theatre audiences, performed her one-woman show about Joyce Grenfell here, while Dame Judi Dench's late husband, Michael Williams, gave his one-man show about the seventeenth century diarist and author, John Aubrey, whose Brief Lives was a classic of its time.

The Novello Theatre, opposite the Duchess and south of the Theatre Royal, was until recently called The Strand, but was given the more glamorous – and theatrical – name The Novello – by its owner, Sir Cameron Mackintosh. Ivor Novello lived and died in a flat above the theatre, as is recorded by one of London's many blue plaques by the flat's entrance door, next to a bus stop.

Ivor Novello's life would have been easier had he stuck to public transport. His insistence on travelling from the flat to his country house by Rolls Royce, (inadvertently) breaking petrol rationing rules, saw him sentenced to a month's imprisonment in 1944. He, like Gielgud (who was only fined) survived the potential disgrace and professional ruin, for he was always a hugely popular actor and the sentence was widely seen as over-the-top for the nature and scale of the offence.

The Novello is used as a London base for the Royal Shakespeare Company but also stages straight shows and musicals from a variety of other companies and producers.

On the other side of the Waldorf Hotel (whose palm court was given the same design as that on the ill-fated Titanic), is the Aldwych Theatre. William Terriss's (see the ghosts chapter again!) daughter, Ellaline, was performing here the day her father was murdered by a deranged actor at the stage door of the Adelphi. Miss Terriss was a great beauty, as was another actress who will always be associated with The Aldwych – Vivian Leigh.

Miss Leigh, who in real life was also Lady Olivier, played one of the great roles of her career here. She was later to say that the role, that of Blanche DuBois in Tennessee Williams' classic

New Orleans drama, A Streetcar Named Desire, tipped her into madness, due to the emotional strain of playing a woman whose mind is going when she, Vivien Leigh, suffered from bouts of manic depression in her own life.

These bouts finally ended the otherwise fairytale marriage that linked her to Laurence Olivier in the public mind for some twenty years (they had been linked privately for longer). Throughout the 1940s and 1950s this pair were theatre royalty, whose overseas tours were like thespian versions of real royalty, with local dignitaries coming out to meet them, cheering crowds at railway stations: the works.

The Aldwych was for many years, between the wars, the home of a string of comedies by Ben Travers. Collectively known as the Aldwych Farces, they entertained Londoners during the heady years of the Roaring Twenties.

From the 1960s, for some 20 years, the Aldwych was home to the Royal Shakespeare Company, who then moved to a purpose-built new London base in the Barbican, in the City of London – the old Square Mile which was the original London, and which is still in effect a City-state within the capital.

Other landmark productions at the Aldwych have included a memorable production of Edward Albee's Who's Afraid of Virginia Wolf? co-starring Dame Diana Rigg and David Suchet, as well as David Hare's Amy's View, starring Dame Judi Dench. Another of the West End's select group of Dames of the British Empire is of course Dame Maggie Smith, who co-starred with Richard E Grant in Oscar Wilde's brilliantly witty late-Victorian comedy, The Importance of Being Earnest. In complete contrast, the most recent (and hugely profitable) show at the theatre is Dirty Dancing – the stage musical version of the Patrick Swayze hit movie.

Another A list (in both senses of the letter) theatre is the Adelphi, which has a Jessie Matthews bar in the basement. This is a tribute to a gamine star of the 1930s British stage and cinema, whose lithe body, comic timing, sweet voice and sexy stage and screen presence made her a huge star. One of her biggest hits was Evergreen, which was performed at the Adelphi which was later made into a successful film, too.

Jessie Matthews was plagued by even worse mental health problems than Vivien Leigh, and had a famously uneven private life, running off with Sonnie Hale, the husband of fragrant (and very popular) Evelyn Laye.

The 1930s seem to live again at the Adelphi, not just because of the Jessie Matthews bar but because the theatre (a Victorian construction) was given a make-over in the 1930s, and looks like a classic Art Deco cinema inside.

One of the Adelphi's major hits was some 50 years later, in the 1980s, with Me and My Girl, which made a fortune for the young man who re-wrote the original book of the musical. That man was Stephen Fry. Another beneficiary of the show's success was a young actress called Emma Thompson, while the leading man was Robert Lindsay, who far more recently played the title role (originated by Laurence Olivier) of The Entertainer, in John Osborne's devastating metaphor for the decline of post-war Britain.

Entertainment has been the name of the game for The Adelphi in the last couple of years, with the lead role for a revival (at the Adelphi) of the Andrew Lloyd Webber/Tim Rice musical Joseph and the Amazing Technicolor Dreamcoat. The young man chosen to play the part of Joseph was picked by the nation after a long and highly enjoyable television contest between a dozen or so good-looking and talented young musical theatre actors.

Youth seems to impregnate the Donmar Warehouse, a small playhouse, created by Sir Donald Albery and Dame Margot Fonteyn (hence its name, an amalgamation of theirs). As a theatre it punches way above it's weight and however distinguished the actors and writers who work there, there does seem to be something perennially youthful about the place, which gives it another layer of appeal to audiences.

The Donmar's glory days seemed to be in the 1990s under Sam Mendes, who went on to develop his theatre career and establish a cinema one (his American Beauty was a stunning debut), but after he left the theatre was entrusted to Michael Grandage, who initially continued also to programme Sheffield's Crucible Theatre, too!

Grandage has beaten the odds and done equally as well as Mendes, while proving himself to be one of London's leading theatre directors as well as a great artistic director of the Donmar. Although he no doubt has a long time to run at the Donmar, when he does eventually go he will be a very hard act to follow, and the Donmar will be amazingly lucky if it can manage a hat-trick of brilliant appointments.

The Vaudeville Theatre is a small playhouse, on the north side of The Strand, between the Adelphi and the Lyceum Theatres. Like all central London theatres it has hosted a vast number of plays down the years, as well as many musicals. American movie star Macaulay Culkin appeared here in Madame Melville, and won over Londoners who had initially wondered if an ex child star Hollywood actor could hack it on stage in the capital city of Theatre.

The Vaudeville's musical connection includes Julian Slade's Salad Days, which was seen by a young child who fell in love, not just with the show but with theatre in general, and announced to his parents that when he grew up he wanted to be a producer. That little boy became Sir Cameron Mackintosh and the rest, as they say, is history! Mackintosh helped change the face not just of West End musical theatre but of Broadway's too, thus ensuring his place in history – and a stunning fortune estimated at several hundred million pounds.

The Lyceum Theatre, near the north end of Waterloo Bridge, belonged (literally, as he owned it) to the actor-manager Sir Henry Irving through the last three decades of the 19th century. Irving is unknown to the general public today but he was a huge star in Victorian times, and among his most ardent admirers was Oscar Wilde.

Another writer associated with Irving was the actor's business manager, Bram Stoker, who is now far more famous than his employer, thanks to the runaway success of his horror novel, Dracula.

In his own day Irving had an unparalleled public reputation as an artist, which is why he was the first actor ever to be knighted – by Queen Victoria, in 1895. Irving's leading lady (and sometime lover) was Ellen Terry, the great-aunt of Sir John Gielgud. Terry's name, along with Irving's and Stoker's, is engraved on the back wall of the now restored theatre.

The Lyceum closed in 1939 and was due to be demolished but after the war it was taken over and used as a dance hall for many years, though some sense of theatrical connection was maintained thanks to performances of the Mystery Plays, directed by Bill Bryden.

Andrew Lloyd Webber bought the theatre, restored it and saw it reopened in 1996 (the date is marked by a roundel on the front of the theatre, to the side of the impressive portico) with a production of the Lloyd Webber/Rice musical Jesus Christ, Superstar.

Other theatres on the edge of Covent Garden are The Shaftesbury – which is just on the north side of the area's boundary – The Garrick, The Duke of York's, Wyndham's and The Noel Coward.

The Noel Coward belongs, like The Novello, to Sir Cameron Mackintosh, who renamed it from the Albery – which it had been named after a London theatrical dynasty. Before being called The Albery it had been called The New. This was a joke that stuck. The theatre was built by Sir Charles Wyndham, who first created Wyndham's Theatre (which backs on to it) and then, after some years when the current theatre was a building site, decided to build his new theatre: hence the name.

As The New, the theatre was the wartime base for Laurence Olivier and his company, and also saw many ballet productions, including Sir Robert Helpmann's dance version of Hamlet.

In 2008 and 2009 Wyndham's was the base for the Donmar Warehouse's West End season: of Ivanov, starring Kenneth Branagh, Twelfth Night, starring Sir Derek Jacobi, Madame de Sade, starring Dame Judi Dench and Hamlet, starring Jude Law. Law is best known these days as a movie star but began his acting career on the London stage, most notably in Les Parents Terribles, which opened at the National Theatre before transferring (re-titled as Indiscretions) to New York, in a production where Law was the only actor in the cast to cross the Atlantic to Broadway.

The Shaftesbury's latest hit has been the stage musical version of Hairspray, in which the Divine role in the movie was played by Michael Ball, an actor and singer with a huge following. His career began in yet another Lloyd Webber Show – Aspects of Love – and has blossomed ever since. Unlike the Shaftesbury, which has had many ups and downs and was considered by some to be an 'unlucky' theatre. Hairspray fortunately changed all that…

The Garrick is an attractive theatre on the Charing Cross Road, almost opposite the National Portrait Gallery and the statue of Sir Henry Irving next to it, the sometime manager and star of the Lyceum Theatre, whose career has been touched on earlier in this chapter.

Garrick was the eighteenth century actor-manager who ran Drury Lane before finally passing the playhouse on (for ready cash) to Richard Brinsely Sheridan, the playwright-turned-theatre owner who, despite earning his fortune from the stage, saved his greatest passion for politics, becoming a Member of Parliament.

His wife, Elizabeth Linley, was a beautiful and talented singer but her husband insisted (in a very un-bohemian way, more appropriate to a businessman than a writer of great stage comedies) that she must give up performing in public once she became his wife, so that they might be a more respectable couple.

The Duke of York's Theatre is another small playhouse, whose real moment in theatre history came in December 1904, when, two days after Christmas, James Barrie's Peter Pan had its premiere and a literary phenomenon was born – s sort of Edwardian Harry Potter. The theatre tends to stage plays rather than musicals, because of its size, and Tom Stoppard's plays seem to suit it, with a revival of his Arcadia (first seen in the West End at the Theatre Royal, Haymarket) taking place there in 2009.

The histories of all these theatres can only be touched on here (each could fill a book in itself, with Drury Lane needing more than one volume) but as can be seen, Covent Garden can certainly claim to be the heart of London Theatre, even if its soul does seem to move from one area to another, depending on the cultural and commercial currents. The term 'West End' certainly includes Shaftesbury Avenue, but the centre of Theatreland remains Inigo Jones' piazza and the theatres and opera houses that surround it.

'Shut up Arnold, or I'll direct the play the way you wrote it."

John Dexter to Arnold Wesker.

'If any play has been produced only twice in three hundred years, there must be some good reason for it."

Rupert Hart-Davis

Floral Hall

The Royal Opera House

Garrick Theatre

CHAPTER THREE

FORMER RESIDENTS OF COVENT GARDEN

With the exception of David Garrick, whose house is still to be seen in Southampton Street, there are not many visual signs left where many of the most famous people lived in Covent Garden, several centuries ago. Ellen Terry lived for a time, above the theatre bookshop, in Cecil Court, so I feel it is more relevant to describe some of the personalities who lived there in the last century. Others are mentioned throughout the book.

James Agate lived in Grape Street, just off Shaftesbury Avenue, and was London's most famous critic for many years. As famous as one of his successors, Kenneth Tynan, was, when he was a drama critic. A grand bon vivant, James Agate was well known for his taste in wine at the restaurants mentioned in this book. He began writing for the Manchester Guardian, then in the Sunday Times in 1923. As his notoriety grew he became overconscious of his own personality. He wrote his nine-volume selection from his diary 'Ego: 1932-1947' and a biography of Rachel, the great French actress, also twenty volumes of his essays and reviews. George Bernard Shaw wrote that only things that are written down on paper survive, and perhaps that is why James Agate is still very much remembered today. His diaries proved to be records of hundreds of theatre productions during those years, and he describes his own personal tastes and day to day living experiences as well interesting anecdotes about his daily life. It is a pity that the other people in this book didn't bother to record some of their daily lives.

In his 1926 book. "A Short View of the English Stage" he writes...

"A large part of the London scene is given up to plays about dope fiends and jazz-maniacs.(So what else is new?) Other large tracts are abandoned to the inmates of musical comedy. Roughly speaking, three fourths of the London stage is closed to persons possessed of the slightest particle of intellect or the least feeling for the drama."

Alan Dent born in 1905 lived in Covent Garden for fifteen years, five of them in a Long Acre garret and ten in an attic in King Street. He was a young man when he came to London from Glasgow.One of the largest influences in his life was when he worked as an assistant and secretary to James Agate, for over fifteen years. He also ghost wrote for him at times. Dent was a London theatre critic of the old Manchester Guardian and later of the News Chronicle. For twenty one years he was film critic of the Illustrated London news. He wrote biographies of Mrs. Patrick Campbell and Vivien Leigh. He also was closely associated with Laurence Olivier's outstanding Shakespearean films, Henry V, Hamlet and Richard 111, as text advisor and script editor. He wrote that it must be part of the Londoner's innate and almost mysterical perveresity to have decided to call the quarter 'Covent Garden' instead of Convent Garden, an old garden of the monks of Westminster Abbey which stretched from Long Acre to the Strand.

From his earliest years Dent had a passion for the theatre and not inclined to play with his schoolmates unless he could induce them to play at play-acting. He writes that he once saw Sarah Bernhardt when he was 8 years old and. fell asleep, so he didn't know whether he had been a good critic or a bad one.

He writes that "Covent Garden was part of my very nature, and for one of my Bohemian character it is the very core of London, just as Mayfair is the core of London for the man -about -town, and just as the East End is the only end that matters to a true

Cockney. I belong to Covent Garden and find myself in it every time I go to London."

He became friends with many people in the theatre, and maybe because he was a critic he was invited several times to go to the Opera House with these people. John Gielgud invited him to go with him to see Maria Callas sing in Bellini's "Norma". Later on he saw her again at La Scala in Milan when she sang in Verdi's "La Traviata", and had a 'momentous luncheon' with her the next day. On another occasion he met Sir David Webster walking in the Market and David invited him to the Opera that evening to hear Handel's "Samson", and during the final twenty minutes there "glided on to the stage, like a stately swan," a new Australian soprano to sing "Let the Bright Seraphim" with a supernatural brilliancy, It was the now-historic first appearance on the Covent Garden stage of Dame Joan Sutherland.

He also tells of his saddest theatrical experience of any kind when he saw Kathleen Ferrier singing Gluck's "Orfeo" and making what was her last appearance on any sort of stage. "She sang nobly and serenely to the very end of her part. It was a triumph of sheer volonte over physical agony. It was the last time she sang."

Sir John Barbirolli answered a letter from Dent saying that it was a solemn privilege to conduct that night for his beloved Katharine which brought us so close to the final tragedy. And these words from Sir Neville Cardus, her great friend and great critic..

"That she was taken from us in her full rose and prime is grievous yet, nearly beyond the scope of philosophy to bear as brave in the face of vicissitude as she was happy in all weathers. Her personal qualities even transcended her art: for great as she was as a singer, she was greater still as Kathleen Ferrier. Not since Ellen Terry has any artist been so universally loved."

Opposite the Opera House entrance, is Broad Court next door to the Bow Street Police Station and Law Courts. In this wide pedestrian walk way, you find some historic houses on your left, and a quaint hotel called Fields on your right. William Wycherley, the Restoration playwright lived here, as did Henry Fielding the playwright. Three famous actors Charles Macklin, Wroughton and Lewis…the latter, not to be confused with Lewis Casson, acted at Covent Garden for over 36 years. The front doors in Broad walk signfiy the residences of long forgotten actors who worked for scores of years in these two great theatres. It is just a short walk from the Lyceum Theatre which was the theatre where Henry Irving's great partnership with Ellen Terry, thrived..

Here is an account from Ellen of their first meeting.

"One very foggy night in December 1867, I acted for the first time with Henry Irving. This was a great event in my life, but at the time it passed me by and left 'no wrack behind'..Until I went to the Lyceum Theatre, Henry Irving was nothing to me and I was nothing to him. I never consciously thought that he would become a great actor. He had no high opinion of my acting. He has said since that he thought me charming but as an actress hoydenish!"

However another wrote that he had seen a young fellow act and if he doesn't come out as a great actor I know nothing of the art. This was none other than Charles Dickens who was clearly more perceptive than Ellen Terry herself was.

Sir Bronson Albery died in July 1971 at the great age of ninety. He owned among other theatres both the New and Wydham's which stand back to back between St. Martin's Lane and the Charing Cross Road. During the year 1973 the name of the New was happily changed to the Albery as a tribute to his memory. This must have gratified the great old man, and he would have been no less gratitfied to know that the play still successfully running when the New became the Albery was a revival of Dion

Boucicault 130-year old comedy “London Assurance”, in which Sir Bronson’s famous step-father Sir Charles Wyndham, used to enjoy playing the charming adventurer called Dazzle.

Thackeray, the great novelist and London-lover (1811-63) enjoyed and revelled in Covent Garden as much as – probably more than – all the countless porters and salesmen, and club members, writers and painters, actors and draughtsmen. Men about and around the town and the theatre, who for the past three hundred years have worked and played and lived there to the top of the hilt. It was Thackeray who, in a superbly comprehensive passage, caught the place’s very essence.:

‘The two great national theatres on one side,; A churchyard full of moldy and undying celebrities on the other; a fringe of houses studded in every part with anecdote and history; an arcade, often more gloomy and deserted than a cathedral aisle: A rich cluster of brown old taverns – one of them (The Garrick Club?) filled with the counterfeit presentments of many actors long since silent who scowl or smile once more from the canvas upon the grandsons of their dead admirers; a something in the air which breathes of old books, old pictures, old painters, and old authors; a place beyond all other places one would choose in which to hear the chimes at midnight; a crystal palace- the representation of the present- which peeps timidly from a corner upon many things in the past; a withered bank that has been sucked dry by a fabulous clerk; a squat building with a hundred columns and chapel-looking fronts, which always stand knee deep in baskets, flowers and scattered vegetables; a common centre into which nature showers her choicest gifts, and where the kindly fruits of the earth often choke the narrow thoroughfares; a population that never seems to sleep, and that does all in its power to prevent others sleeping; a place where the very latest suppers and the earliest breakfasts jostle each other on the footways – such is Covent Garden Market, with some of its surrounding features”.

Clemence Dane, famous novelist, prolific play and screen writer, painter and author who was a close friend of Noel Coward is almost forgotten now. Her real name was Winifred Ashton. She took the pen name from the Church in the Strand, St. Clements Dane.

She was a large woman, whose photographs show her dressed in long flowing robes and shawls, which may not have been her daily clothes, but certainly made her look slightly out of the ordinary. She wrote several best selling novels, including 'The Flower Girls", screen plays for classic films, such as "St. Martin's Lane" which starred Vivien Leigh, Rex Harrison and Tyrone Guthrie, also "Bill of Divorcement" and 'Will Shakespeare".

She lived in Tavistock Street, opposite the old flower market in Covent Garden for thirty years and wrote a book about it. She writes

"The years went by, from the early twenties up to the war and on till the middle fifties. All the while I had been getting an education that money could not buy. Somebody told me that Kean had once lived in my rooms; that led to looking up biographies of all the people he in turn had known and the Victorians led back to the Regency, and back-and back- till I was in the Elizabethan age, and Covent Garden was a meadow again. After a while I also found out that living in the Market had a queer effect on one's sense of period. It must be that time is unstable in any district where opposites meet as they do in the Garden: country and town, commerce and romance, art and cabbages, magic and money, not to speak of past and future. Indeed, I wonder if any other plot of ground in the world, except perhaps the Forum in Rome, gives the passer-by such a happy sense of being alive at one and the same moment in all periods of a city's history, or of being jostled by crowds of invisibles who share the garden with you. They co-exist with you. They prickle on your skin like electric sparks on a frosty morning as they pass you, alive in their own time-space and busy on their own- important lively affairs."

Walking through Covent Garden in the footsteps of Garrick, Irving and Kean, Ellen Terry somehow you will find that their spirits will enter your bones. Spend time finding these old places and revive their memory.

Noel Coward wrote in his diary that if he had been away out of England, as soon as he reached London he would dash over to Clemence Dane's flat to catch up on all the latest news and gossip and take refuge there during the blitz and during the war. Her meals were legendary and often she would give him a dozen eggs and perhaps a bowl of flowers, floating in a large bowl, so that it was always difficult to descend the stairs without spilling the water everywhere.Her flat was always filled with writers, artists and actors discussing the latest news in the theatre in London. Coward invited her to stay with him in Jamaica at Blue Harbour several times, where she spent her days painting in the garden while Coward wrote in his studio.

When war broke out, she had been warned by the street Warden that it was her duty as occupier to see that everyone in the house went down to the cellar when the siren sounded. "But could I get the men down into the cellar? They were amendable enough when I called. They came politely down the ladder into that queer retreat with its smell of rats and roses and its flowers standing in pails all over the damp bricks, but they wouldn't stay down. One morning after a particularly noisy night I passed the wholesaler flower shop on the corner. There were no flowers in the window, but a sign said "Business as Usual".

During those years, Clemence was fortunate enough to be invited to some rehearsals at the Opera House, and she was delighted to watch Zeffirelli rehearsing Don Giovani as well as John Gielgud when he directed an opera there. She said that the actual auditorium is wonderful when it is empty and that the interpretation of a work is always slightly different than when the house is full. She also described going to the ballet there, to watch Fonteyn and Robert Helpmann, and later on Nureyev. She attended the last night of the Royal Ballet season when Fonteyn and Nureyev received 22 curtain calls…they took longer than the actual ballet. She said she would queue up for the Opera but not for the ballet. Former Prime Minister John Major's wife, Norma, queued up too, but for the Opera. She wrote a biography of Dame Joan Sutherland, but in her early days, she would even sleep out overnight to get tickets to hear her sing, joining the queue the night before.

Clemence wrote her own book about living in Covent Garden and decribes the spectacle of watching the truck drivers unload flowers and vegetables below and the noise of them shouting to each other starting at the crack of dawn. She must have had nerves of steel to have stayed there for so many years. Also during the Second World War and helping out whenever she could.

Most of the theatres stayed open, and the late Judy Campbell said that it was how she first met Noel Coward…during a raid. A bomb fell on the Savoy Hotel but only did minor damage, Coward was dining there at another table from Judy, and to keep things going, he got up and started to sing, and asked if there was anyone else who would like to join him. He spotted Judy, and the rest is history.

She sang for him and shortly afterwards became his leading lady in several of his plays. She introduced the song 'A Nightgale Sang in Berkely Square" I digress here to put in a note about Judy. That song made her famous, and it became her signature song for the rest of her career. I had the privilege to hear her sing it many times, the last time in New York at the Cabaret Convention at the Town Hall.

Maybe I am being sentimental, but to me, she epitomized the spirit of the British, during World War 11. Working in London during the Blitz, she also toured all over England during the war, and survived to tell the tale. She said the reason Coward put his hands down her bodice onstage one night, was to keep them warm. So there she was still tall, elegant and beautiful at the Town Hall that night still singing. She was the star of the evening. Her turn came just before the final curtain. Sheridan Morley gave a short introduction, then the pianist started the first chords, on the concert grand piano, downstage left, and she slowly entered from the other side of the stage, her long wonderful evening stole draped over one shoulder the end of it trailing along behind her, the applause lasted until she had crossed the stage and sung the first note, beside the piano. You could hear a pin drop for the total duration of her act as everyone knew that they were listening to a great star, now in her eighties. Later that night, she was toasted at dinner at the Algonquin where she surpassed everyone with her wit and conversation well into the small hours.

I had invited her a few years previously to take part in "Love from Shakespeare to Coward" the anthology of verse, prose and anecdotes, which we first performed at the Theatre Museum and the National Portrait Gallery in London then the night after the Cabaret in New York, in the Oak Room at the Algonquin Hotel.

Clemence Dane knew all that generation and wrote plays for them She wrote 24 plays and 40 novels, as well co-writing several others with an Australian writer.

ANGUS MCBEAN .Lived on Endell Street

Today not many people remember the famous photographers who immortalized all those legenday stars of the theatre when they were at the pinnacle of their careers. Fashion photographers are often written about, their work exhibited but few theatre photographers are remembered except perhaps with a retrospective at the National Portrait Gallery in London.

Angus McBean was a giant in the West End theatre scene when it was at its most golden. His photographs adorned practically every theatre's exterior display cases with scenes from the play being presented inside. Not only did he photograph the stars acting onstage, but he did portraits of these stars in his studio.

His photo of Vivien Leigh is a classic which is featured in a book about his work which was published several years ago.

Every actor wanted to be photographed by Angus McBean, as a photo by him impressed casting agents and producers, when you first left drama school and were looking for a job.

I was no exception. I will never forget my visit to his studio in Endell Street just after I had graduated from the Guildhall.

It was one of those small row houses, still there in the middle of Endell St. I rang the door bell and was lead up to the first floor by a young man, into a kind of dressing room, which was next to the studio and in it was a curious looking antique polished-wood cabinet in one corner. He opened it for me and then left the room. It contained a porcelain basin, three way mirrors, little lights over them, tiny little drawers, hooks and silver fittings. I presumed it was there to help you tidy your hair, refresh your makeup or whatever. I waited in the room for ages in complete silence, except for a clock ticking somewhere. It all seemed so mysterious but at the same time rather glamourous, I felt that maybe Mr. McBean had left the premises, driven away by this client he had agreed to photograph, or maybe he had a hidden camera or a peephole in this tiny room and was watching me analyzing my face to find my bad side.

Finally he appeared and we went into the studio. One week later I picked up the proofs and chose my first professional photograph.

Cecil Beaton called him the best photographer in the country; Lord Snowden declared him a genius. It is no exaggeration to say that Angus McBean revolutionized portraiture in the 1930s, or that he immortalized the likes of Audrey Hepburn, Marlene Dietrich and Elizabeth Taylor. Blending wit, drama and fantasy with the consummate skill of a master photographer, without a doubt Angus McBean has been one of the greatest influences on theatrical, portrait, creative and commercial photography in the last 100 years.

In 1925, after his father's early death, Angus moved with his mother and younger sister to Acton in West London. He took a job in the antiques department of Liberty's where he learned to restore, and indeed to make, antiques. His spare time was devoted to mask-making and photography in a rudimentary studio and darkroom at home, and to theatre-going in the West End. He invested in a 'magnificent' half-plate Soho Tropical reflex camera that was cased in mahogany and brass. 'In those days, the bigger the negative, the better the quality of the final print and the easier to retouch'. He used it, along with hard Zeiss lenses and Kodak Panchromatic black-and-white plates, for nearly twenty years. 'I never knew what focal lengths they were or what film speeds were. I just knew what they could do for me.'

After seven years he gave up his job at the department store, grew his distinctive beard to symbolize the fact that he would never be a wage-slave again, and began to win recognition as a maker of theatrical props. Among his early commissions were intricate pieces of medieval scenery for John Gielgud's 1933 production of Richard of Bordeaux and some much praised masks for an Oxford University Dramatic Society production of Doctor Faustus and a West End play, Ballerina. Since this was a time when decorative wall masks were much used in fashionable interiors, his masks were much used in fashionable interiors, his masks of luminaries such as Greta Garbo and Lloyd George were also chronicled in social columns. While he was giving a small exhibitions in Mayfair of masks and a few photographs, the leading Bond Street photographer Hugh Cecil admired his striking portraits.

Through them McBean received his first photographic commission in the theatre in 1936. Ivor Novello had ordered some masks for a play - The Happy Hypocrite - in which he was starring with a new and very beautiful young actress, Vivien Leigh. The matinee idol so liked the romantic photographs that McBean took in order to make his masks that he commissioned him to take a set of production photographs as well. The results, taken on stage with McBean's idiosyncratic lighting, instantly replaced the set already made by the long-established but stolid Stage Photo Company. McBean had a new career and a photographic leading lady: he was to photograph Vivien Leigh on stage and in the studio for almost every performance she gave until her death thirty years later.

In 1985 Angus McBean achieved fame of a more formal kind when his earliest studio portrait of Vivien Leigh, his favourite picture, was turned into a postage stamp.

He died in 1990.

GBS At a performance given by an Italian string quartet, Shaw's companion remarked approvingly, "These men have been playing together for twelve years."

"Surely," said Shaw, "we have been here longer than that."

(Shaw lived at Adelphi Terrace..just south of the Strand for many years.)

The Garrick Club

Garrick's house in Southampton St. (2009)

CHAPTER FOUR

RESTAURANTS IN COVENT GARDEN

There are so many unusual and good restaurants in Covent Garden it is difficult to know where to start. The most historic are the theatrical places which are still in business.

RULES is first, because it is the oldest restaurant in London (1799), and one of the most famous of all of the theatrical restaurants. I have already mentioned the fact that the Prince Regent courted the actress Lily Langtry in a private suite on the first floor...their dinners still remembered by a little alcove on one of the private dining rooms upstairs. It is said that the second front door, was built to enable the Prince and his guests to enter through a private entrance. The list of famous guests is legendary and the private dining rooms are named in their honour. There is the Graham Greene and the John Betjeman dining rooms and the hallways leading to these rooms are filled with photographs and letters of many celebrity actors and writers who have dined here. I suppose you might call it London's equivalent to Sardi's in New York...except of course, it is much older.

Every time I dine there I feel, especially in the main room, the spirits of all those writers and artists who have dined there at the same tables. It is a rather astonishing fact that the same kind of food is still served there, as they had a century ago. Steak and Kidney Pudding...with vegetables and rich gravy, is always a speciality as well as their Steak and Kidney Pie...served under puff pastry and ringed with a white paper crown. Critics who have criticized the food, have no real feeling for what Rules has known for centuries, the house dishes are the courses to order.

Today the second entrance, the door to the right, no longer used for Royalty, is for the regular clients who have a special card to enter the door, to use the staircase up to the cocktail bar on the first floor. This saves them having to pass through the main dining room to get to the second floor.

The Ivy, on West Street is again rather too famous now because it is so difficult to get a table without a reservation. The atmosphere has changed somewhat since they removed the carpeting which deadened the noise, and put in wood floors, which carry the sound, so you don't get that quiet intimate atmosphere that The Ivy used to have, now it is rather more upbeat with lots of young business types. However if you are a sentimentalist you might want to dine there for old times sake, because it once was a rather simple place. When Noel Coward first went there, it was little more than a simple Italian trattoria, with linoleum on the floor, and checked tablecloths. The owner gave him credit. Then when he made it famous, it was the place to go and have lunch after the opening night of your play, or by a friend of yours, to either drink to celebrate or drink to commiserate if the notices were bad. Coward went there after a disastrous first night at the nearby Phoenix Theatre, of his new play "Sirrocco". The audience had booed him at the curtain call, and spat at him at the stage door, where a crowd had gathered, as he left the theatre. We know that many playwrights and actors still remembered this. Judy Campbell, one of Coward's leading ladies, recalls when Coward invited her to lunch there with him one day. She wrote that it was a wonderful lunch and he asked all about her and her career plans. Then he said 'Where's the jam?" She thought he was asking for some kind of pudding. He explained that during the lunch he had talked all about her and now it was time for her to compliment him and show some interest in his work…"Everybody needs some jam, Judy" and she never forgot the advice.

Mon Plaisir, 19-21 Monmouth Street is London's oldest French Restaurant and has for over fifty years been family owned. Established by the Viala brothers during the forties, it was acquired by the Lhermitte family in 1972. There are four dining rooms, and all feel completely different and regulars have their favourite room where they will always ask to be seated. They boast that they have one of the best cheeseboards in London. The cheese is brought back from France every week.

I have heard from many people that they think that this is the best French restaurant in the area...if not London. The menu is traditional and they usually have a three course theatre menu, which is served early and usually includes their house specialities. It is the place where you do hear French spoken, and most of the staff are French, so you if you enjoy French cuisine, this is the place. Celebrities of course, have signed photos there and many of them often return when they are in London...so you just might see your favourite French chanteuse. The chef who sometimes appears describes the menu du jour.

Joe Allen's....another theatre place, which is owned by Joe Allen, has restaraunts in Paris and in New York. It is frequented by actors and dancers especially if they are working near by as there are numerous theatres and the Opera House of course, just up the road. Joe has a weird sense of humour because the walls in his establishments are covered in theatre posters of shows that were box office failures. There are many. There is a theatre dinner menu, reasonably priced and last time I was there, the food was excellent. Service has been always good, and it is always crowded at lunch times. I recommend reservations here, and that goes for the other places mentioned also.

Savoy Grill...hopefully they will keep the atmosphere as it was, however since the renovation when all the original furniture was sold off, it remains to be seen if it will be as elegant and glamorous as it once was. The old days of having your food presented and served from under a large silver cover maybe gone for good.

Salieri's...in the Strand. Next time there is a heatwave in London, when all the restaurants are over heated, try the basement dining room at this place, as well as the wonderful sea food they specialize in when you eat downstairs.

Porters' Steakhouse on Henrietta Street. Here you will find good steaks but also the old traditional dishes from Dicken's time. . Try the chicken pot pie or the Shepherd's pie which is as delicious as their steaks. Owned by an aristocrat who may not want me to name him, you can buy a copy of the history of his family tree in the restaurant when you dine there. It has been a fixture for many years, and is very popular with the residents of Covent Garden.

Sheekey's Fish Restaurant. Although not really in Covent Garden as it is on the other side of St. Martin's Lane, in St. Martin's Courtyard between the Lane and Charing Cross Road, it boasts the most excellent fish dishes in the area. The walls all full of old photos of the celebrities who have dined here and recently they opened a new room next door to the original restaurant which is an Oyster Bar in the evenings.

Clos Maggiore, King Street. This must be the prettiest restaurant in Covent Garden, both inside and out.. It has a romantic interior, with branches of flower blossoms, overhanging the tables, and masses of flowers everywhere. The menu features all the classic Italian dishes and the service is excellent with many little extra touches that make up a good restauarant. It is relatively new, if you consider Rules, near by, or the cofee house, Boswells, on the other side of the Piazza. But their reputation is growing and reservations are strongly advised, especially for lunch.

Bertorelli's. This is a favourite of opera and theatre-goers in the area. It was one of the first Italian restaurants who catered to the performers as well as the audience. Close by the Opera House, the staff are used to seeing their favourite tenor drop by for a plate of their famous pasta. A good place to dine when going to see a Rossini opera perhaps.

Somerset Maugham:" At dinner one should eat wisely but not too well, and talk well, but not too wisely.

"The cook was a good cook, as cooks go, and as good cooks go, she went."......Saki.

Rules Restaurant

Clos Maggiore

Mon Plaisir French Restaurant

CHAPTER FIVE

COVENT GARDEN'S UNIQUE SHOPS

Covent Garden can claim not just its theatrical heritage but a treasure-trove of unique shops. The Garden has attracted shoppers since it was first laid out by theatre designer and architect Inigo Jones in the 1630s. Today's descendants of these early emporia are idiosyncratic, amusing, stylish, chic – above all, unpredictable.

Covent Garden became defined by the fruit and vegetable market that stood at its centre for centuries, but that has long since departed south of the river (to an area called Nine Elms) and the area has, for some thirty years been one of London's greatest tourist attractions, bursting with life and vitality. Given this, it's not surprising that enterprising shop owners, from the major national stores to quirky local ones, should pitch their tent there.

The following is a selection of those to be found, but there will inevitably be others that readers will discover for themselves.

Penthaligon Perfumery.
Wellington Street.

Established in 1779 this is one of the oldest and most distinguished perfume shops in London. It was a favourite of the film diretor, Visconti, and now also his protégé, Franco Zeffirelli., who always pays them a visit when in London. The shop is filled with exotic perfumes and creams, not found anywhere else.

Fox's makeup shop
22 Tavistock Street.

This is a shop that is inextricably linked to the theatre world. Founded in 1878, Fox's used to be primarily a supplier of costumes to the theatre and film industries. Much of their stock was eventually sold to Angel's in Shaftesbury Avenue (just north of the borders of Covent Garden) as the company decided to focus on makeup, which had originally been a sideline rather than the main area of expertise.

The shop specializes in all sorts of makeup and also provides workshops on how to choose and apply it. As theatre lighting techniques have improved, so has the sophistication of makeup, and this is reflected in the style and range of products on offer in Tavistock Street.

The Tea House
15A Neal Street

What could be more British than a cup of tea? The Tea House, founded in 1982 offers a wide range of teas, from the stimulating to the soothing, from the reassuringly recognizable to the exotic. In fact there are some 70 types of tea available! Tea accessories – cups, saucers, tea pots, are all for sale, too. The only thing you can't do is drink the tea on the premises, but then Covent Garden has more than enough cafes for those who can't wait to get home to have a 'cuppa'.

Tea was at first an expensive novelty, which arrived some decades after coffee had become Londoner's drink of choice, but if swiftly won over everyone from Queen Anne to street labourers. It is only in the last twenty years or so that coffee has fought its way back to pole position, but tea remains a very English beverage, whose apotheosis is to be found in the classic Afternoon Tea.

Royal Opera House Gift Shop
Bow Street

For many people Covent Garden doesn't mean the Piazza and its surrounding network of streets and alleyways, shops and restaurants: it means the Royal Opera House.

Opera and ballet companies need all the cash they can get, so the ROH has its own shop, selling CDs, DVDs and a variety of merchandise. From coffee mugs to T shirts, from dance magazines to books on opera, histories of each company and biographies of the great performers who have graced the ROH's stage – such as Callas and Nureyev – the shop has something for every fan.

Especially good value are the posters, mostly for Royal Ballet productions, which feature stunning photos of dancers. One of the company's leading principals, Ivan Putrov, also has his own set of postcards, made up of production shots from a range of ballets.

Pleasures of Past Times
11 Cecil Court

David Drummond's shop in Cecil Court is a wonderful tribute to past theatrical performers of every sort – from clowns to chorus boys, divas to dancers, opera stars to stand-up comedians.

The shop seems almost like a time machine, with the benevolent and immensely knowledgeable Drummond standing benignly at the controls, ready to take the shopper back to the world of Edwardian London, with it Gaiety girls and young stage door Johnnies, or to Henry Irving's Lyceum, where the first actor to be knighted forged a lasting stage partnership with Ellen Terry, the great aunt of 20th century stage and screen star Sir John Gielgud. It is said that Ellen Terry lived upstairs in this building for a time.

Cecil Court is like something out of the book/play/film 84 Charing Cross Road – a collection of antiquarian book shops that give an idea of the Old London that so many tourists come to find, but which can prove curiously elusive to those who don't know where to look. Here are wonderful antique shops with astonishing wares on show.

Porcelain, china, silver, marble, jewelery and all are a collector's dream.

Dress Circle
57 Monmouth Street

Another must-see shop is Dress Circle. This specializes in musical theatre and has an unrivalled collection of CDs and DVDs, along with cards and other memorabilia, celebrating the world of showbiz. It also has (downstairs) books on musical theatre, along with music scores.

The shop has been one of the landmarks of Covent Garden for some 30 years, and its staff are amazingly knowledgeable about their subject. Dress Circle also functions as a sort of news service for the musical theatre community, with a large notice-board plastered with posters of forthcoming and current shows – especially cabaret. Although New York definitely has the edge over London in terms of cabaret performances, there is a thriving and growing cabaret culture in London, too, and this is the place to find out what is on and where.

Moss Bros
27-29 King Street

Moss Bros (Londoners pronounce it Moss Bross) is the most famous men's clothes shop in London, thanks to a unique feature: as well as selling clothes, it also hires them out.

The shop offers evening clothes and formal wear for hire, and is an inevitable stop on the way to Buckingham Palace for those who are being presented with an honour by the Queen and who want to wear the correct formal morning wear but who wouldn't dream of actually buying an outfit they will only ever wear once. Similarly, for people attending weddings.

The shop was earlier just across the road, on the site now occupied by Tescos supermarket. The hire section is right at the back of the shop which is otherwise stocked with the latest in men's upmarket fashion, with a wide range of suits, shirts and blazers as well as all the usual accessories.

Australia Shop
27 Maiden Lane

Maiden Lane is one of the quaintest little streets in Covent Garden, and contains not only London's oldest restaurant – Rules – but the stage doors of the Adelphi and Vaudeville theatres. A surprising place then, to find a shop celebrating all things Australian – especially as the most Australian area of London is undoubtedly Earl's Court, quite some way West.

But then that is one of the attractions of this area – the unexpected and the mix of old and new. This is the place for homesick Australians to come and buy food and other products (including clothes) that remind them of home. Britain may, as the famous quip has it, have lost an Empire and not yet found a role, but as a city it retains echoes of its Imperial past, and the Australian shop is a reminder of the colonial links that still bind the city with far-flung corners of the globe.

Stanfords
12-14 Long Acre

Stanfords is London's premier map shop, with an astonishing collection of maps, atlases and guide books to every part of the world. The shop often hosts lectures and events to do with travel and given the Royal Geographic Society's recent decision to cut back on funding expeditions, Stanfords is in effect the headquarters for all intrepid explorers who want to head off to relatively unknown areas of the world.

Stanfords also has it own coffee shop – Café Copia – in which to pore over your purchases and from whose comfortable chairs you can plan (or fantasize) your own travels across seas and mountains.

Wow Retro
14 Mercer Street

As its name implies, this is a clothing shop that specialises in retro clothing, boots, shoes and accessories – for men and women. It also has some items of furniture, so if you want to emulate 1960s singing superstar Dusty Springfield in the song 'Going Back' and try to recreate the past, then this is a good place to start!

Blackout II
51 Endell Street

Another retro shop for the nostalgically minded in Blackout II on Endell Street. Clothes range from the 1920s to the 1980s. There's nothing new about liking old clothes and mixing them with new (think of all those red Victorian army tunics that young men seemed to wear in the late 1960s) but then that's the point of this shop: to enable today's customers to enjoy the fashions of the past but also to feel free to use them in conjunction with modern fashion, to create something unique. They say that all cats look grey in the dark, but at Blackout you get to shine!

Nauticalia
18 Covent Garden Market

Founded in 1974, Nauticalia sells all things nautical and is a celebration of life at sea – or on the river. The Thames is the reason why London was built and, as Churchill once said, runs like a silver ribbon through its heart, but its all too easy to forget the river, and the sea to which it leads – in a city that generally seems to look away from the river banks.

Nauticalia, a few hundred yards north of the Thames, in the heart of Covent Garden Market, brings a welcome reminder of the cool of the river and the salt tang of the sea, with its mixture of nautical replicas (from lamps to diving helmets, from ships' models to signs, bells and bosun's whistles.

The Covent Garden shop is the company's flagship but it also makes nautical objects for sale in museums, seaside shops and other outlets: a business that won the Queen's Award for Exports in the late 1990s.

Segar and Snuff Parlour
27A Covent Garden Market

The Davy's wine bar chain's Covent Garden showcase is The Crusting Pipe (the name refers to the process of making a type of port), which is found in the basement area of Covent Garden Market. One floor above, on ground level, is the Segar and Snuff, a small and very atmospheric shop which sells cigarettes, cigars – and of course snuff!

A real taste of old London, its combination of masculinity and Victorian charm would have suited Colonel Pickering, Henry Higgins' friend and helper in My Fair Lady, the classic musical whose opening scene was a stone's throw from the shop, under the portico of St Paul's, Covent Garden: the actors' church.

Thomas Neale's
Earlham Street

This ground and basement shopping development has a range of shops, one of which specializes in surf wear – not a sport that you immediately associate with London!

The development is named after Thomas Neale, who created the adjoining Seven Dials area that includes Dress Circle, the musical theatre shop. The area was named after the streets that radiate off the sun dial (restored in the 1990s and reopened by the Queen of the Netherlands) that is the centrepiece of Seven Dials.

Thomas Neale's is a very modern attractive, air conditioned complex centred around an attractive café and situated at the side of one of Covent garden's most attractive and influential small theatres, the Donmar Warehouse. In that respect, it's a little like the famous advert for the Victoria and Albert Museum back in the 1980s, which described the V and A as 'an ace caff with quite a good museum attached'!

Shoe Master
24 Bedfordbury

This small shoe repair shop fills a vital role for any visitor to London who spends time walking its streets. It also happens to be in an attractive old-world building at the Bedfordbury end of Covent Garden's most historic and attractive little alleyway, Goodwin's Court.

This alley contains some of the oldest houses still standing in central London – the bow-fronted windows let the light into a row of tiny houses that date from the late 1690s. Goodwin's Court is the site of the office (at 14A) of the legendary theatrical literary agent Peggy Ramsay, a powerful and charismatic woman who was immortalised on film by Vanessa Redgrave in a film about one of her best-known clients, playwright Joe Orton.

Penthaligon Perfumery

Pipe Shop in Piazza

Mark Sullivan Antiques & Decoratives

Musicians in Piazza

Dress Circle Shop

Stanford's Book Shop

CHAPTER SIX

HISTORIC ESTABLISHMENTS...... COVENT GARDEN PUBS

The Salisbury
St. Martin's Lane

Named after the Victorian Marquess of Salisbury who served as Foreign Secretary and as Prime Minister, this is one of the best examples of Victorian pub architecture to be found in central London. The family name of the Marquesses of Salisbury is Cecil – hence nearby Cecil Court, with its collection of bookshops. The family, which has been at the heart of the British Establishment since William Cecil became Queen Elizabeth I's most trusted advisor, still owns the freehold of the land on which the pub is built.

The Salisbury was one of London's best-known gay pubs and, not entirely co-incidentally, theatre pubs, until the mid 1980s. Since the theatre crowd moved out and the gays moved on, the pub has lacked the personal atmosphere that it used to have, but it is still a wonderful architectural throwback to High Victorian taste, with lots of brass, wood and glass – only the Red Lion in St James's comes anywhere close to the Salisbury in this respect.

The Salisbury used to have a lovely open fire, which was both welcoming and charmingly authentic, adding to the Victorian atmosphere. In recent years the Health and Safety culture of modern England has meant that the fire has remained unlit. This is made all the more regrettable by the positioning, above the now cold hearth, of a picture of a Victorian family celebration – in a room with candles burning brightly. We can but hope that, as customs change, one day the Salisbury will once again warm its winter visitors, not just with port or brandy, but with an open log fire.

The Opera Tavern
Catherine Street

Opposite the Theatre Royal, Drury Lane, the Opera Tavern dates from the 1870s and

is another good example of Victorian pub architecture, especially on the outside. Upstairs is an attractive function room that is often let out for private parties. The pub, along with the nearby Nell of Old Drury, is popular with theatre workers who don't have far to travel for a much-needed drink once the curtain comes down.

Nell of Old Drury
Catherine Street

Originally called The Lamb, and subsequently the Sir John Falstaff, this pub is named after Nell Gwynn, one of King Charles II's most popular mistresses (with the public as well as the monarch), who acted in light comedies at the theatre opposite.

There is reputed to have been a secret tunnel that ran from the pub, underneath Catherine Street and into the Theatre Royal, allowing the King to pay private visits to the young actress. This is a charming story, but in reality the King would have attracted just as much unwanted attention by walking into an inn as he would by simply arriving at the stage door!

Nell Gwynn Tavern
Bull Inn Court

Another pub named after Nell Gwynn, this is tucked away in an alleyway, Bull Inn Court, named after a previous pub, long-since demolished. The Nell Gwynn has a brief written tribute on panelling outside the pub, with a summary of her career, including Samuel Pepys's famous reference to 'pretty, witty Nell' at Drury Lane.

A very small pub it nonetheless has a dedicated clientele who make full use of the jukebox, though the television screens may not be to the taste of those in search of an older, secret London – soccer matches and a beguiling sense of history don't really go together very well.

That apart, this alleyway, like the others that link the ancient Maiden Lane with the Strand, has a real sense of Old London, especially in a winter twilight.

The Cross Keys
Endell Street

A beautiful pub in Endell Street, that runs from near the Shaftesbury Theatre in the north to close to the Royal Opera House in the south.

The Cross Keys is famous for its floral frontage - a mass of climbing plants and flowers that really come into their own each summer, in a blaze of colour. Above this display are cherubs carrying the crossed keys of St Peter – a traditional symbol of the papacy. Another such decoration can be found on the corner of Endell and Shelton Street – a small statue or bust of the Virgin Mary – a sign of the ancient Mercers Company, one of the great Livery companies of the City of London, who own the building on which, as tradition decrees, the representation of Mary symbolises their ownership.

Inside the Cross Keys, the walls are also covered – though with paintings, posters and photographs, rather than religious iconography, which might otherwise detract from the serious business of having a pint!

The Nag's Head
James Street

The Nag's Head is a Victorian pub but stands on the site of much older predecessors – the first pub on this site reputedly dates from the early 1670s, when the Covent Garden area was still relatively young.

James Street is a busy thoroughfare that gets very crowded in summer, not least because the presence of a row of 'street sculptures' and entertainers means that passers-by stop to look and block the narrow street and pavements: it's said that James Street is therefore one of the most densely-packed in London.

The Nag's Head offers a refreshing sanctuary from all this, and is also an ideal watering-hole for visitors to the neighbouring Royal Opera House: part of the Nag's Head fronts Floral Street, where the ROH's stage door is located. A good place, then, to look out for the stars.

Lyceum
The Strand

The Lyceum Tavern is named after the nearby theatre, home for some thirty years of the Victorian actor Sir Henry Irving, the first actor to be knighted.

Though the pub pays some tribute to the theatrical connection, its main business is beer, as is made clear by the vast barrel that hangs from its frontage, on the Strand, near Waterloo Bridge (scene and title of a 1940 weepie starring Vivien Leigh and Robert Taylor).

The Lyceum's unique feature is the little wooden booths where couples or small groups of friends can settle themselves and court or chat undisturbed – a rare chance in London's normally crowded and occasionally jostly pubs. This gives an intimate –conspiratorial even, atmosphere to the place: shades not just of Waterloo Bridge but of Noel Coward's Brief Encounter.

The Lamb and Flag
Rose Street

Nestling beside the modernistic HQ of the Society of London Theatre, the Lamb and Flag is one of the oldest pubs in Covent Garden, dating back to the 1670s. Upstairs is the Dryden Room, named after the poet and playwright, while downstairs you could almost be in a country pub rather than the heart of London.

This is a tribute to the Lamb and Flag's unreconstructed sense of place and time – this is where people come to drink and chat and recount office gossip. It is not, despite its location, a theatre pub, but that simply adds to its sense of authenticity. Unusually for a central London pub of its antiquity and literary connections, this is a meeting-point for local residents and workers rather than tourists, so anyone in search of 'real' London is more likely to find it here than most other such places.

Maple Leaf
Maiden Lane

The Maple Leaf, located in historic Maiden Lane, close to Rules restaurant, is a Canadian-themed pub that is very popular with locals as well as expat Canadians. The Canadian High Commission is a few minutes' walk away, the far side of Trafalgar Square.

Sports coverage on television screens ensures a packed pub, especially at the weekends, while those to prefer to just drink and soak up the atmosphere, as well as the beer, can admire various North American mementoes, from ice hockey shirts to native Canadian artifacts. A little outpost of Empire in the heart of the Mother Country!

The Wellington
The Strand

Situated next to the Lyceum Theatre, the Wellington makes a speciality of its fish and chips – and what could be more British than that?

The pub is named after the British general, the Duke of Wellington, whose London address at Apsely House had the wonderful address of Number 1, London! The Duke swapped a military career for a political one, serving as Prime Minister from 1828 to 1830.

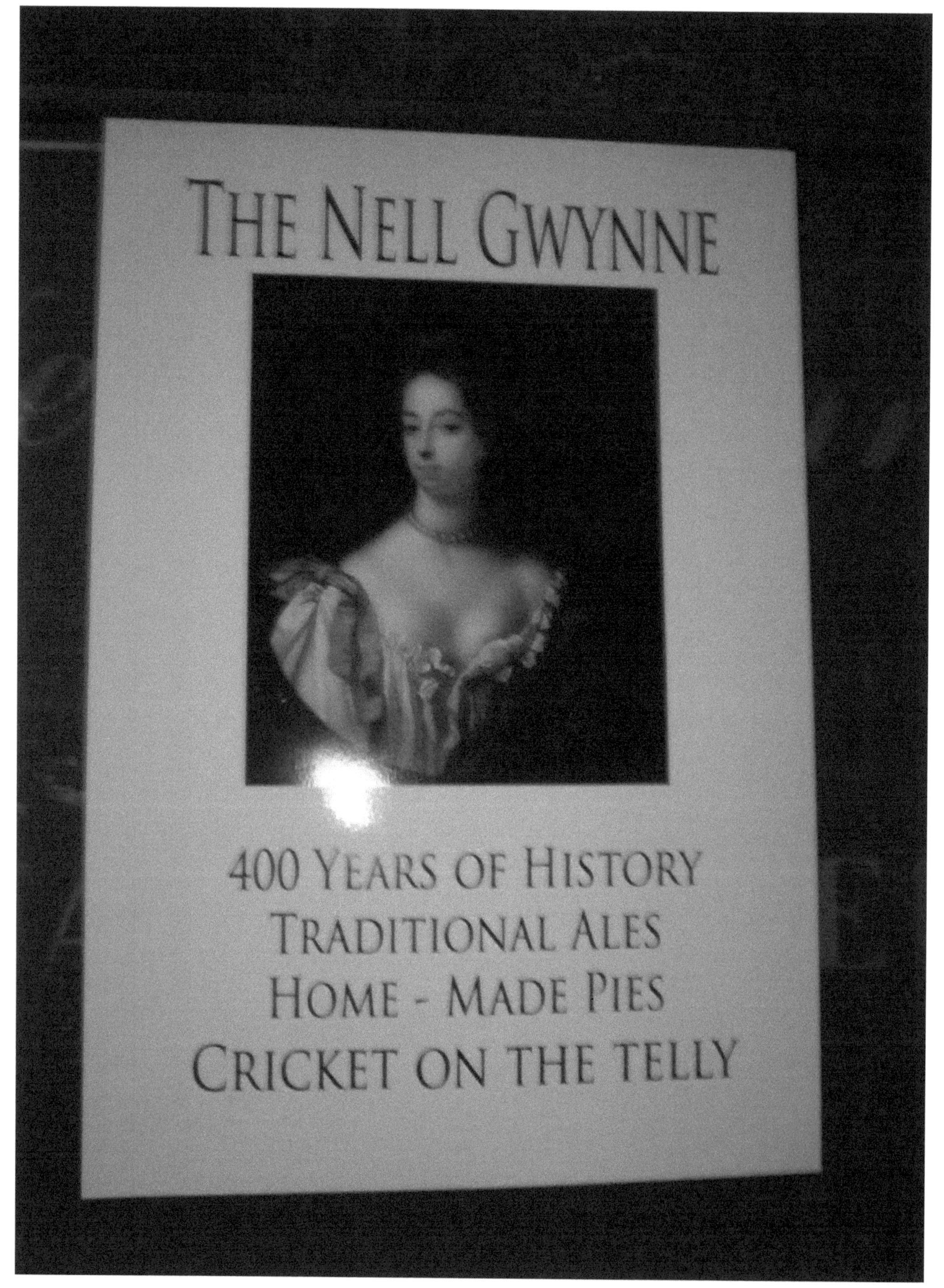

Nell Gwynn Pub

Lamb and Flag Pub

The Nag's Head

CHAPTER SEVEN

SPECIAL PLACES OF COVENT GARDEN

The Royal Opera House and the Crush Bar.

One of the crown jewels of the West End's crown, the Royal Opera House today dominates Covent Garden Piazza, a legacy of the massive redevelopment at the turn of this century (from 1996 to 2000) that saw a number of Georgian buildings pulled down – against significant local opposition – to make way for the current site.

Even the most vociferous critics seem to have been silenced by the end result, which is a superbly restored opera house with the best back-stage facilities in Europe, if not the world, and superb front-of-house areas, including the Floral Hall, which is the most beautiful bar area in all London.

There have been several theatres on the site of the current Royal Opera House, two of them destroyed by fire. In the early 19th century there were two months of rioting when prices were raised to pay for the replacement building, a year after the disastrous conflagration of 1808.

In a sense, the issue of prices has never gone away: people still feel that the cost of opera and ballet tickets (opera tends to be more expensive, especially when a world-class star is flown in) are very high, but equally it can be seen as a mark of prestige to be able to afford such elegant surroundings: as a result, the Royal Opera House is a popular venue for corporate entertaining – which may be one reason that Royal Opera House patrons are so much better dressed than in most theatres!

The Royal Ballet predates the Royal opera, and the two companies, which share the building's stage and rehearsal facilities, have often vied for pole position in terms of cultural reputation and commercial success. Both companies had a golden period in the 1960s, when Franco Zeffirelli staged his stunning production of Tosca, starring Maria Callas, while the Royal Ballet were invigorated, along with their leading ballerina, Margot Fonteyn, by the arrival of the fiery young Russian star, Rudolph Nureyev, fresh from his dramatic defection in Paris. Today the Royal Ballet makes much (quite rightly) of its guest star Carlos Acosta, whose magnificent physique and technical skill has attracted a new generation of ballet fans. The spirit of Nureyev still haunts (in the best possible sense) the Royal Opera House, with a large photograph of him standing in the wings, a reminder and inspiration to today's dancers.

The Royal Family's association with the Opera House continues in the form of Prince Charles, who is a devoted patron of opera. His previous wife, Princess Diana, was very much a fan of the ballet, as was an earlier generation in the form of Princess Margaret, whose long and loyal connection with the Royal Ballet is commemorated in a plaque near the site of the old Crush Bar, by the grand staircase that leads from the ground floor to the Floral Hall.

The Queen Mother also used to enjoy the ballet and was taken to the Royal Opera House by her daughters to celebrate her birthday – on other occasions they would take her to a West End show, but in any case the main point was to give her the chance to enjoy a night out at the theatre.

The Royal Opera House stage door, in Floral Street, is a very modern looking affair, but it is the gateway to a building which, along with its predecessors, is the repository of an extraordinary amount of stage and musical history, with names as varied and distinguished as Handel (for opera), Kean (for drama) and Grimaldi (the great clown) all being associated with the site.

The Crush Bar, on the first floor of the Opera House has been the scene of Royal Receptions, cocktail parties, concerts and recitals. It was always the place to meet before the performance, but now with the new restaurants elsewhere in the complex, it is used for special events and recitals. It is one of the most elegant rooms in Covent Garden.

There are many dramatic stories connected with the Opera House including the cancellation of divas, postponements, farewell performances, curtain calls that last up t0 30 minutes, cat calls, boos, and always the press have some new scandal. Dame Joan Sutherland made her farewell performance here and she once remarked that instead of an audience booing, a deathly silence, after the end of an aria, is much more damning.

Hitchcock in Henrietta Street

Alfred Hitchcock may have been America's favourite film director but he was born an Englishman and the son of a greengrocer who traded with the Covent Garden market. His first successful film, a serial killer thriller called The Lodger (1926) featured the back alleys and passages behind Fleet street, where the newspaper presses were located in those days, and in one of his last films, Frenzy (1972) he was able to pay tribute to the area where his father earned his living – Covent Garden. In particular, the film deals with Henrietta Street, the thoroughfare named after King Charles I's wife then widow, Queen Henrietta Maria.

The film is about a serial killer who murders women with his tie – and frames one of his friends in the process. The murderer is a Covent Garden worker, and the film, which included plenty of outside shots of Covent Garden, was, partly, the great director's tribute to the market place that everyone knew was going to close and whose traditional sights and sounds would be lost forever.

Henrietta Street is prominent in the story as the killer (a Mr Rusk, played by Barry Foster), has a flat at number 3, Henrietta Street, and is seen loading a sack, containing the body of a strangled woman, onto a lorry-load of sacks of potatoes.

As well as the film connection, their was a literary one, in that the distinguished publishing firm of Victor Gollancz (which published George Orwell) was located here. However, it is Henrietta Street's link with Alfred Hitchcock that has earned in some small immortality, as the director saved its old uses for posterity in Frenzy. Incidentally, it was appropriate that the screenwriter for this film was Anthony Shaffer, the playwright whose greatest hit Sleuth, was premiered two years earlier, in 1970, at a Covent garden theatre – the St Martin's, which is itself now the home of Agatha Christie's murder mystery The Mousetrap. This is a string of coincidences and connections worthy of Hitchcock himself!

On a final note (pardon the pun) on the director and Covent Garden, a biographer of Hitchcock, Patrick Mcgilligan, has suggested that Hitchcock hoped to have a scene in a movie (that was never made) in which a leading diva, belting out an aria on the stage of the Royal Opera House, would see a man being stabbed in a box and end her aria on a piercingly high shriek of horror. A brilliant idea, like so many of his, and a shame that we never got to see it realised on celluloid.

The Hospital

Covent Garden was the site of many hospitals, the best-known of which was Charing Cross Hospital, on the north side of the Strand, opposite Charing Cross – the official centre point of London. Today Charing Cross hospital is a major West End police station, though the infirmary's name lives on in another hospital of the same name, in Hammersmith.

The Covent Garden Hotel (see hotels chapter) was built in the converted shell of a hospital dedicated to the needs of French citizens in London – whose numbers were significantly swelled by the emigres who arrived here after the French Revolution in 1789 and the Terror that ravaged Paris in subsequent years.

The Hospital (or The Hospital Club as it is officially called) is also, as its name suggests, a converted hospital building, but this is a private members club for people involved in the creative industries – film, television, art, theatre, dance. You are likely to rub shoulders here with movie stars and members of the Royal Ballet, along with the occasional rock star.

The traditional London clubs (ie gentlemen's clubs) are to be found in the St James's area, mainly along Pall Mall and St James's Street. The Hospital, by contrast, is an example of a far more up-to-date and creative members club, aimed at a younger demographic.

It opened some five years ago, and was founded by Paul Allen (of Microsoft) and David Stewart (of pop group The Eurythmics). It was an almost immediate success, not least because it combines creative business (recording studios, edit suites, meeting rooms) with pleasure – bars, restaurants and chill-out rooms for just relaxing.

It also has a fabulous art gallery space, which has shown work by wall-sprayer extraordinaire Banksy, who was given a joint exhibition with the late Andy Warhol.

The Hospital is a classic case of urban regeneration, as well as reflecting the historic creativity and style of the area in a modern, innovative way.

The London Transport Museum

Think of any city and you think of symbols: Paris has the Eiffel Tower, Pisa has a leaning one. Rome has the Coliseum, New York the Empire State (or, for some, the Chrysler),

wearing a crown, of course. And then there's the big red bus. Think of London and you'll have several images to choose from: Big Ben, the Tower of London, St. Paul's Cathedral, Tower Bridge. Or perhaps simply the Queen – double-decker bus that is far, far more than a prosaic moving platform for getting around the city – it's a symbol of the city itself.

The London Transport Museum, which also looks at the Underground, at trams, at horse-drawn buses and other vehicles, realizes the continuing appeal of these machines, and has one cannily placed outside the entrance, in the Piazza, to help attract the tourists.

London's previous mayor, Ken Livingstone, phased out the old Routemaster buses (with their hop-on, hop-off open platforms) but the modern replacements are still red, and most double-decked. The single deckers, or 'bendy buses' never found a place in Londoners' hearts, and will apparently be removed by Livingstone's successor, Boris Johnson.

The Transport Museum goes back to one of the earliest forms of public transport – the Sedan Chair. This was a little box in which the customer sat. Handles at the front and rear were designed to be carried by the pedestrian equivalent of taxi drivers. They were more comfortable than walking, not least because the streets were so filthy in the 17th and 18th centuries when these chairs were used.

The modern day equivalent, which can be seen on the streets (look out for them as they hurtle past in exuberant fashion) rather than in the museum are bicycle rickshaws, where young men (usually foreign students) use pedal power to get delighted tourists from one part of central London to another. Though be warned – they're not cheap!

Taxis are another London icon, and there are examples of the changing shape that these have had since the first motorized ones appeared in Edwardian times. Other displays at the museum include the wonderful range of posters that decorated tube stations between the wars, and were an art form in themselves.

Bow Street Police Station

The Bow Street Runners were the precursors of the modern London police force, which was not established until the 1820s, in the face of a storm of protests about the perceived threat to civil liberties. The Metropolitan Police was nevertheless established, when Sir Robert Peel was Home Secretary (ie Minister of the Interior). This is why police were known as Peelers or as Bobbies. The latter name is still in use, as is the phrase 'The Bobby on his beat' – a beat being the area of streets which the individual policeman had to patrol.

The current police station was put up in the 1850s and closed early in the 21st century. There has been some uncertainty as to its future. A police museum was one suggestion but it is more likely to be turned into a luxury hotel.

Adjoining the police station is the Magistrates' Courts, which closed only a couple of years ago, and which were always very busy. An easy way of identifying whether any celebrities were appearing to answer for relatively minor misdemeanors (drunk and disorderly, for example) was the presence, early in the morning, of a cluster of paparazzi.

The Magistrates' Courts were sometimes used for theatrical performances, especially in the days of the Covent Garden Festival, a summer event when theatrical, dance and music productions were held in a wide range of buildings within the

Covent Garden area. A very popular show in the Courts was a production of Gilbert and Sullivan's Trial By Jury!

Sainsbury's

England's best known supermarket began its life with a modest single shop in Drury Lane, opened by John James Sainsbury and his wife in 1869 and specialising in low-cost but good quality produce. The chain now has some 800 outlets and members of the Sainsbury family have used the wealth that flows from this for a variety of public service projects, including the magnificent Sainsbury Wing, the modern extension to the National Gallery on Trafalgar Square. The Sainsbury Wing replaced the original architectural plan, which was memorably described by Prince Charles as being like a 'monstrous carbuncle' on the face of an old friend.

An even closer Covent Garden connection is that Lady Sainsbury, wife of Lord (John) Sainsbury, is the former ballerina, Anya Linden. They are great patrons of the arts, with a particular fondness for the Royal Opera House, of which Lord Sainsbury was Chairman for four years and the work of the Royal Ballet. The couple were awarded a medal for arts philanthropy by the Prince of Wales. Their charitable trust has given over £20 million to the arts, while Lady Sainsbury has founded a biannual award for stage design.

Robert Morley once met an old friend at the Garrick Club, fellow actor Llewellyn Rees, whom he had not seen for some time. "It's nice meeting old friends," said Rees warmly. "A lot of people think I'm dead."

"Not if they look closely," said Morley.

Goodwin Court.

Looking toward Bedfordbury ... A ghostly walk.

CHAPTER EIGHT

COVENT GARDEN'S GHOSTS

As you would expect with such a historic area of central London, Covent Garden has its fair share of ghosts. Many of these are associated with the theatre, and as the heart of London's modern-day Theatreland, Covent Garden understandably lays claim to some of the capital's classiest spooks.

The epicentre of supernatural activity is the Theatre Royal, Drury Lane, which is the oldest theatre site (still in current use) in London. The first playhouse was erected here in the 1660s, soon after King Charles II returned from exile and brought the theatre with him – Cromwell and his Puritans having banned it during the years (1649-1660) when England was a republic.

The most famous of the many ghosts is The Man in Grey – a spirit that walks from one side of the auditorium to another, clad in a grey cloak, and wearing an eighteenth century-style tricorn hat on his head.

The ghost is supposed to bring good luck to actors who see him. Unusually, he is seen during the day, though daylight (the ultimate enemy of ghosts and vampires) never penetrates the auditorium, of course.

The legend of the ghost has lasted for centuries, and was given some scientific backing when, in the course of building refurbishment - an ongoing process in a theatre which has also been completely rebuilt several times. The current theatre is the fourth on the site. Workmen discovered the bricked-up skeleton of a man with a dagger in his ribs – and the remnants of clothing that matched the description of the Man in Grey.

Other ghosts that belong to Drury Lane include that of Dan Leno, the music hall star, and Joseph Grimaldi, the clown. As with the Man in Grey, they are supposed to be happy spirits – Grimaldi in particular is said to offer a ghostly hand to actors who lose their way on stage – a ghostly take on Noel Coward's famous aphorism that actors' main concern shouldn't be their motivation but to remember their lines and avoid bumping into the furniture!

A ghostly smell of lavender is another often-mentioned phenomenon at Drury Lane, and has been variously attributed to Dan Leno and to the ghost of a gay theatregoer who, in his declining years, wore lavender sachets to hide the smell of his incontinence when trying to chat up young actors!

The smell of flowers is appropriate to female ghosts, given the marvellous bouquets that actresses – and ballerinas – are presented with on stage, not to mention those given to visiting royals. Given that ghosts tend to be associated with sadness rather than joy, it would not be surprising to hear of sightings of the spirit of Princess Diana, who loved to go to the theatre – though to see ballet rather than plays.

At a gala performance in the 1980s, at Covent Garden's other opera house, the London Coliseum, of Onegin, the John Cranko ballet about a Russian aristocrat who is haunted by his past, and troubled by mental images (if not an actual ghost) of a poet he killed in a duel, Diana appeared on stage to congratulate the cast. The ballerina presented the princess with her own bouquet, saying "Tonight, all my flowers are for you!"

Were Diana to appear at the Coliseum or the Royal Opera House (where, after all, she danced on stage, in a surprise birthday tribute to Prince Charles), she would be following in the footsteps of others who have returned to the theatre after their death.

The Coliseum is haunted by the ghost of a First World War soldier who is seen in the higher levels of the auditorium, from whose cheap seats (which used to be simple wooden benches) he enjoyed himself on leave from the battlefields where he would eventually meet his death.

The Coliseum, like all theatres, can seem very creepy when the audience has left, and the firemen who patrol the place at night are happier checking the stalls and dress circle than the areas frequented by the lonely spirit of the doomed soldier.

One of London's most famous ghosts met his death not on a battlefield but the steps of his own stage door. William Terriss was a leading Victorian actor, whose manly good looks and strong stage presence made him a favourite with a generation of female theatregoers. Terriss's downfall was that he ran his own company of actors as well as performing on stage, and one of these men, Richard Prince, was mentally unstable.

Having been fired by Terriss, he vowed to take revenge, which he did on 16 December 1897. Challenging Terriss as the actor arrived at the theatre for that day's performance, he raised first his voice and then his hand – in which he carried a dagger. He viciously stabbed his sometime employer who fell to the ground, bleeding to death.

Terriss's ghost has been seen at the Adelphi but also, curiously, at Covent Garden tube station. Well, curious until you learn that Terriss used to buy snacks at a cake shop at the station, and presumably prefers to haunt somewhere with happy associations rather than the place where his brilliant career came to an abrupt and bloody end.

Speaking of tube stations, tourists might be forgiven for thinking that the (now disused) Aldwych tube station is haunted, given the number of figures wearing period costume that can be seen, from time to time, flitting around the entrance. These, however, are not spirits but the very corporeal manifestations of actors: the station is a favourite location for film-makers.

Unlike the Tower of London, or places like Smithfield meat market, where large numbers of people met grisly ends (Smithfield was where heretics used to be burned to death in front of cheering crowds), Covent Garden is a place associated with pleasure – theatre, shopping, restaurants, pubs and bars – a selection of which are looked at in other chapters. It's ghosts therefore confine themselves to theatres rather than the street or old houses and (unlike the spirit at the Dominion Theatre, in Tottenham Court Road, which is an apparently malevolent one that has scared numerous actors) tend to be kind rather than sinister.

Today the best-known ghost in Covent Garden is The Woman In Black, who scares audiences witless eight times a week at the little Fortune Theatre. The play is a stage adaptation of Susan Hill's novel, and has theatregoers literally jumping in their seats with fear. So if it's ghosts you're after, then one at least can be guaranteed to make an appearance – for the price of a theatre ticket!

CHAPTER NINE

COVENT GARDEN HOTELS

Given its many attractions and ideal location for access to the City and the West End, its not surprising that Covent Garden should have a range of hotels to choose from – or that they are as fascinating and rich in history as the streets in which they are located.

THE FIELDING HOTEL
Broad Court

The Fielding is situated in Broad Court which, despite its name, is modestly proportioned. Broad Court is close to the Royal Opera House (about a minute's walk away!) and has a charming statue of a ballerina at the point where the Court meets Bow Street.

Bow Street was where the famous Bow Street Runners were located. They were an early sort of police force, many years before the creation of a recognisable modern police for the capital, and they were the brainchild of two brothers, Henry and John Fielding.

The hotel, which has a more intimate atmosphere than many of its larger competitors, is named after Henry Fielding, the writer whose best-known novel is Tom Jones, a rollicking 18th century novel that was filmed in 1963 with Albert Finney in the title role.

Fielding was also a playwright (specializing in satires) and worked as a magistrate, alongside his brother John, who was blind – a legacy of an accident in his teens. The brothers made a formidable pair, and John was no less effective for being blind – it was said he could recognise all the most regular offenders who appeared in his court – by their voices!

The Fielding is a charming oasis and a place for those who want to enjoy the sense of history that these little streets and courtyards have to offer, yet can be a couple of minutes from the heart of the action.

COVENT GARDEN HOTEL
Monmouth Street

The Covent Garden Hotel occupies the site of a former French hospital and indeed Covent Garden used to rather specialise in Hospitals (hence The Hospital Club in Endell Street, not to mention Charing Cross Hospital, which is now a major police station).

The hotel is part of a chain (Firmdale) of boutique hotels, and is very popular with visiting American stars, especially those appearing on stage – Macaulay Culkin stayed there, for example, when appearing at the Vaudeville Theatre in Madame Melville some nine or ten years ago.

Many of these stars give interviews (accompanied by PR minders) in the Library on the first floor of the hotel – an elegant book-lined pair of rooms that make a quiet place to talk.

By contrast, the ground floor bar and restaurant has a real buzz, and is one of the smartest and liveliest hang-outs for theatrical and film types in the whole of Covent Garden. The cuisine is excellent and there is a wide range of wines to accompany it.

The rooms are sumptuous, individually furnished and all have very stylish bathrooms.

The hotel has a very attractive screening room and at the weekend there is a film club which shows classic and modern movies. For those of a more energetic disposition there is a gym, and there is also a massage room where tired actors can have the stress of a life on stage smoothed away.

THE WALDORF HOTEL
Aldwych

The Waldorf, part of the Hilton hotel group, is situated between two great London theatres – the Novello and the Aldwych. It is a large and stylish hotel that was given a major makeover a few years ago, when much of its Edwardian opulence was replaced with a more modern decor and feel.

This has been a great success, though some might regret the transformation of the famous Palm Court from a place dedicated to afternoon teas, into a smart bar and restaurant area, however good the food.

The Palm Court was supposedly exactly the same design as the one on the Titanic, which certainly gave a frisson to taking afternoon tea there!

The Waldorf has an indoor pool as well as a fitness centre, so it is a very self-contained place to stay, though it is also ideal for visits out to the theatre – as well as its neighbours, it is a minute or two's stroll to the Theatre Royal, Drury Lane, the Duchess, the Lyceum and the Fortune.

THE STRAND PALACE
The Strand

The Strand Palace may not look very theatrical but it was designed by the father of Jeffrey Bernard, the long-serving Spectator columnist whose extraordinary and alcohol-fuelled life included periods working as a stage hand in the West End. Bernard's career was immortalized, by Keith Waterhouse, in the play Jeffrey Bernard is Unwell – this being the laconic line that the Spectator's editor would place in the weekly magazine when Bernard had been too drunk to file his copy.

The Strand Palace is a favourite with American tourists, which is appropriate given that the Strand Palace was more or less taken over by the American army during the Second World War, as they liked its Art Deco style (designed in 1928 to replace the original Edwardian style). It is very well-situated for access to the theatres and shops of Covent Garden. It has a comfortable bar, the Mask Bar, which is a great place to have a drink before heading for whatever play or musical you have planned for the evening.

A Strand Palace room key was found by war historians in a Western Front trench some 30 years ago, and was given to the Victoria and Albert Museum. The key should of course have been left with the concierge, but it may have been kept as a souvenir by one of the guests who wanted a reminder of London life in the carnage of the battlefields of Flanders. The glass Art Deco foyer has also been saved and is stored now at the Museum. Hopefully it will be on view again before long.

ONE ALDWYCH
Aldwych

One Aldwych is a major boutique hotel that is popular with Hollywood stars and the artistic set on both sides of the Atlantic. It has a beautiful and spacious lobby, which is dominated by the figure of a giant oarsman – appropriate for the forthcoming Olympics!

The hotel has a screening room – naturally enough, given the number of film stars who like visiting here – and two restaurants: Indigo, which overlooks the lobby, and Axis, which is in the basement, and is reached by walking down what has to be one of the most elegant stone staircases in London.

There is also a fitness centre and swimming pool, along with all the state-of-the-art technology you would expect in this class of hotel.

One Aldwych has the added attraction of being very close to Waterloo Bridge – site of a Vivien Leigh movie (Waterloo Bridge), a weepie in which she starred opposite Robert Taylor and ends up, a fallen woman, throwing herself under a lorry.

Today, those who successfully negotiate the traffic around Aldwych and the Strand, can walk across Waterloo Bridge to the National Theatre, the site of much of the best theatre that London has to offer.

ST MARTIN'S HOTEL
St Martin's Lane

Designed by Philippe Starck, this is one of the most manifestly modern hotels in London, from its glass exterior to its minimalist interior.

The hotel is popular with a younger yet moneyed crowd and can seem in many ways more of an American hotel experience than an English one, but its location, next to the Coliseum and opposite the Duke of York's, is ideal for theatregoers. It is also, of course, very close to Trafalgar Square, which increasingly (in the summer) hosts open air relays of live opera and ballet performances from the Royal Opera House, as well as other concert events.

For music lovers the hotel also offers easy access to St Martin in the Fields, the vast church (recently restored to its original beauty) that fronts Trafalgar Square, and which has a great many concerts and recitals as part of its regular programme of events.

The MOUNTBATTEN HOTEL
Seven Dials

The Mountbatten is a boutique hotel in the heart of Covent Garden, with a restaurant/bar whose large plate glass windows look directly onto the dials: a historic feature that seems to be a magnet for tourists and locals alike, who enjoy sitting on its multi-sided base and watching the world go by. Seven Dials is in the middle of a roundabout but a casual visitor would be forgiven for thinking that this is a pedestrianized area, so proprietorial are the people who saunter to and around it, often bearing a glass from one of the neighbouring pubs or wine bars.

The Mountbatten is of course named after one of the 20th century's most distinguished Englishmen. Lord Mountbatten was born a German prince, Louis of Battenberg, but a grandson of Queen Victoria – his mother, Alice, who was one of the Queen's daughters. Louis, born in 1900, grew up in the world of Edwardian royalty, and was fond of his Russian cousins, all of whom were to perish in the Revolution.

His father was First Sea Lord (head of the Royal Navy) in 1912 but resigned during teh First World War due to the strength of anti-German feeling. It was in that atmosphere that the Royal Family changed its name (in 1917) from Saxe Coburg Gotha to Windsor. In the process, all their relatives living in England agreed to give up their German titles, and were given (lesser) English ones instead – Mountbatten went from being a Serene Highness and a Prince to simply Lord Louis Mountbatten.

The hotel commemorates his famous career in the Royal Navy (Noel Coward's wartime film In Which We Serve was based on Mountbatten's exploits) and his role as last Viceroy of India (1946-7). The hotel is close to the Covent Garden Hotel and almost opposite the Cambridge Theatre, where Chicago is continuing its successful West End run, which began at the Adelphi in 1997.

Waldorf Hotel

Number One, The Aldwych.

CHAPTER TEN

....A Walking tour with notes.

A good place to start a walk through this area is the portico of St. Paul's, known as the actors' church. The portico faces onto Covent Garden market --- the central focus of the area, and the reason for its existence. This was originally a convent garden --- the name was gradually altered by generations of Londoners --- that provided fresh vegetables for the monks of Westminster Abbey. Although the monks disappeared with Henry VIII's dissolution of the monasteries in the 1530s, the market remained as a source of food for Londoners, more recently providing vegetables for the smart hotels and restaurants of the West End

The area used to be owned by the Dukes of Bedford whose coat of arms can still be seen on the outside of the market buildings, the latter having now been converted into shops and wine bars, it was a Duke of Bedford who asked Inigo Jones, an architect but also a theatrical producer of sorts (he organised court entertainments, called masques), to build him a church. He specifically wanted a plain church --- "a barn of a place, Jones," --- and Inigo Jones was as good as his word, providing what he claimed to be the finest barn in Christendom !

The portico of the church is what interests us at this point, for we shall enter the inside of Inigo Jones' barn at the end of the tour. The portico is imposing without being ornate, and serves as a perfect backdrop for the street entertainers who are such a feature of today's Covent Garden, and whose ancestors, acting out mystery plays and religious stories, were the founders of modern European drama. The portico has been used to famous effect as the setting for My Fair Lady, one of the longest running shows at the Theatre Royal, Drury Lane, and, subsequently, a highly successful film starring Rex Harrison (reprising his stage performance) and Audrey Hepburn. It is in front of St. Paul's portico that Stanley Holloway, due to be married in the morning, sings his famous request to "get me to the church on time".

Some three centuries before the film, the same portico was the scene of the first ever Punch and Judy show seen in England. The performance was recorded by no less a personage than Samuel Pepys, probably the most famous diarist in history, whose vivid evocations of Restoration London include many accounts of trips to the theatres, together with appreciative remarks on the charms of Nell Gwynn. An inscription (which makes a change from the inevitable blue plaque !) on the church wall records that Pepys saw the puppet show in 1662. There is still a regular Punch and Judy show in the market, but these days it is on the other side of the market. Despite the passage of three hundred years, the happy absorption on the faces of the watching children, and the nostalgic pleasure of their parents, is the same today as it has ever been.

Leaving the portico behind, walk past the appropriately named Punch and Judy pub, through the covered market, to Russell Street. Just before you reach each, look down into the basement courtyard of the Crusting Pipe, the quaintly named wine bar (part of the prestigious Davys group). In the courtyard, seated at the many tables, with a cold glass of white wine, visitors enjoy live music and opera from music students and professional musicians who are continuing Covent Garden's centuries-old traditions of street theatre.

On the left, as you walk down Russell Street, the Royal Opera House has torn down some attractive eighteenth century coffee houses, in order to extend the Opera House and to re-create Inigo Jones' original plans for the area. This has been a highly controversial project, and only time will tell whether this has been an act of vandalism or an enlightened improvement.

The Theatre Royal, Drury Lane

Known in the business as "The Lane", this is the oldest theatre in London (with all due respect to the reconstructed Globe --- see the chapter on The Globe and Shakespeare). As if designed to confuse tourists, the Theatre Royal's entrance is not actually sited on Drury Lane (which runs past the back of the building) but on the less well-recognised (but far more attractive) Catherine Street.

There have been several buildings on the site, a fact explained partly by successive managements' need to increase the size and facilities of the building, and partly because of that perennial London problem in previous centuries --- fire.

The Theatre Royal was established by the granting of a Royal Charter by King Charles II, and this charter, the pride of the theatre, used to be displayed on the cover of every Drury Lane programme, until modern marketing and design did away with it. An understandable change, but an unfortunate loss.

After Charles' father, Charles I, had been beheaded by Oliver Cromwell's regime in 1649, the monarchy had been abolished and with it went the theatre, which was seen as an ungodly and licentious entertainment. When the monarchy was restored with Charles II's return from exile in 1660 (hence the Restoration period of history, usually applied to the years up to his death in 1685) the theatre was restored too.

Despite the King's love of the stage, permission to perform was strictly prohibited, except by licence, given that plays could easily be used for anti-government propaganda. After all, it was following a performance of Shakespeare's Richard II, a play about the deposition of a King, that the Earl of Essex led his ill-fated rebellion against the ageing Queen Elizabeth. The granting of the King's licence was, therefore, vital to respectability and official approval. For many years only two theatres enjoyed this --- the Theatre Royal, Drury Lane, and the Theatre Royal,

Haymarket (see the chapter on West End theatres) hence their names.

The Theatre Royal saw many visits from King Charles, though he was attracted not so much by the plays as by the female players --- another change that he brought about, for earlier in the century, during his father and grandfather's reigns, female parts had been played by teenage boys.

Charles had many mistresses but the most famous, and certainly the most popular, was Nell Gwynn, an actress at Drury Lane. She had started her theatre career as an orange seller, which was something of a cross between an usherette and a prostitute. Graduating to the stage, she demonstrated a talent as a light comedienne and caught the King's eye, and later his heart.

One could write a book on Nell Gwynn alone, but we must move on, leaving her to her place in history, along with all the other ghosts of past performers. Many theatres have a resident ghost, and Drury Lane has a mysterious figure in eighteenth century clothes. Workmen digging away at a wall as part of a refurbishment project found the skeleton of a man, dating from this period, with a dagger in his ribs, so perhaps the ghost story is well founded ! The theatre now owned by Stoll Moss, the largest theatre chain in the West End, organises frequent tours (details from the box office), in which this and many other stories and anecdotes relating to the theatre can be heard.

Of the cast of actors and actresses who have appeared at The Lane, a few should be mentioned. David Garrick, one of the most famous actors ever, who brought to the profession a great talent and a much needed professionalism, ran the theatre with a showman's eye and a businessman's brains, employing all the greatest actors of the age --- particularly the formidable Mrs Siddons. She was an actress of forbidding appearance and a superb tragedienne, particularly in the role of Lady Macbeth. When Sheridan, the brilliant young playwright whose work Garrick put on at Drury Lane, and who took over the ownership of the theatre from him, was asked whether he had ever considered an affair with her, he replied that he would as soon have an affair with the Archbishop of Canterbury.

Sheridan wrote comedies that were quickly recognised as classics : The Rivals, The Critic, and The School For Scandal. Yet despite his success as a playwright, his greatest ambition was to be a politician, and he used his considerable income from the stage in furtherance of a political career, most of which was spent on the opposition benches.

Sheridan was a far better playwright than he was a theatre manager. He spent a fortune on refurbishing the Theatre Royal, only to have it burn down in a catastrophic fire in 1809. The news of the disaster was brought to him during a debate in the House of Commons, but he displayed a typically British stiff upper lip, refusing to have the business of the House interrupted by a personal misfortune. Only after he had finished his contribution to the debate did he feel free to attend to the theatre.

Fire-fighting in those days was more or less limited to stopping the flames reaching adjacent buildings, so there was nothing that could be done to save the theatre. Ironically, Sheridan had had a huge water tank created for just such an emergency, but it had been drained for routine maintenance at the time the the fire took hold --- a typical example of the bad luck that was to dog his time as a theatre owner. As if that were not bad enough, he was not insured !

Even at this moment of crisis, however, Sheridan's famous wit did not desert him. His friends, searching for him amid the confusion and crashing timbers, the flames and the dense smoke, found him at a nearby inn. When asked how he could bear to watch his fortune and his livelihood literally going up in smoke, he simply smiled and asked them, "May a man not take a drink at his own fireside ?"

Although the theatre was, of course, rebuilt, Sheridan was a broken man. His political career fared no better, and he even fell out with the Prince of Wales who, on his father George III being declared insane, was made Prince Regent (1810). There had never been any love lost between George III and his heir ; indeed his legendary distaste of his eldest son accounts for the extraordinary fact of there being two royal boxes at Drury Lane.

The Theatre Royal, Drury Lane, saw many great actors, during the nineteenth century, a selection of whom are represented by busts in the rotunda on the first floor. The man who has the greatest claim to the title, King of Drury Lane, was, however, a twentieth century theatrical phenomenon, Ivor Novello. Ivor (as he was known to friends, family and fans alike) is described in more detail in the chapter on him (see Ivor Novello's London) but it would be helpful to mention, at this point that his string of spectacular musicals saved Drury Lane from closure in the mid 1930s, and ensured its survival for the rest of that decade.

Beginning with Glamorous Night in 1935, and continuing with Careless Rapture (1936) and Crest of the Wave (1937), then finishing with The Dancing Years (1939) he effortlessly wrote, composed and then starred in his own musicals. They owed a great deal to those of Frank Lehar, but they all demonstrate a style that is very much Novello's own. In the year "off", 1938, he decided to ring the changes by playing in, of all things, Shakespeare and, of all plays, Henry V. Given his reputation as a handsome matinee idol and composer of lush, romantic music, the role of the young warrior King (Ivor was forty-five at the time) might seem ill-chosen, and the casting of one of his leading ladies, Dorothy Dickson (a Broadway dancer and noted beauty, with whom he had co-starred in Careless Rapture and Crest of The Wave) as Catherine of France, was unexpected to say the least. A combination of these factors, together with the fact that the Munich crisis took people's minds off the theatre, meant that Ivor's Henry V had mixed reviews and a short run.

Musicals have been a feature of Drury Lane ever since. The long run of My Fair Lady has already been referred to. Miss Saigon, the current production has hit the record books, and among the shows in between was Billy, the musical that helped make the careers of both Michael Crawford and Elaine Page. Despite his later success in Barnum, in Andrew Lloyd Webber's The Phantom of the Opera, and in his enormously popular Las Vegas extravaganza, Michael Crawford is perhaps still best known for his role of Frank Spencer in the 1970s TV sitcom, Some Mothers Do Have 'Em.

The best loved sitcom of them all, Dad's Army, also appeared at Drury Lane in the 1970s, and though not as successful in theatrical terms as it had been on the small screen, it has given a great deal of pleasure to its army of fans.

Leaving the splendid foyer of Drury Lane, and saying farewell to over three centuries of the London theatre that it represents, we walk down Catherine Street past the Duchess Theatre.

The Duchess Theatre, Catherine Street

If the Theatre Royal, Drury Lane represents the venerable history of the London Stage, the the Duchess is an example of a jazz age Art Deco theatre from the late 1920s (very late --- it opened in November 1929) that has survived the vicissitudes of the twentieth century to become a versatile and much liked performing house for revivals and modern plays alike.

Jessica Tandy scored an early success in Children in Uniform in 1932, directed by Leontine Sagan. A rare example (now as well as then) of a woman director, she was later hired by Ivor Novello to direct Glamorous Night just up the road at the Theatre Royal.

Playwrights as varied as Emlyn Williams, J B Priestly, William Douglas Home and Harold Pinter have all had successful shows put on here. Although Oh Calcutta !, Run For Your Wife and The Dirtiest Show in Town all appeared at the Duchess, it is best known for the sixteen years that it was home to No Sex Please, We're British. The Duchess' refusal to be typecast has been shown by the vast difference between three of her latest shows, Don't Dress for Dinner (a farce), Maureen Lipman --- Live and Kidding --- a one-woman revue, and the Royal Shakespeare Company's drama, The Herbal Bed.

From the Duchess Theatre, turn right into Exeter Street. A few yards walk will take you to the junction with Wellington Street and just cross the road from you is the imposing facade of the Lyceum Theatre, recently restored at a cost of several million pounds by the Apollo Leisure Group.

The Lyceum Theatre

There has been a theatre on this site since the 1790s, and it was to the Lyceum that the Theatre Royal, Drury Lane turned for a temporary home after the disastrous fire of 1809. Perhaps the actors brought their bad luck with them, for the Lyceum burnt down too, in 1830. This proved an opportunity for greatly increasing the size of the theatre and the splendour of its appearance, and The Lyceum's elegant facade has been a London landmark ever since.

The theatre's claim to fame rests not in its architecture, but in its association with a giant of the theatre world and the first actor ever to be knighted --- Sir Henry Irving. Hired in 1871 by the Lyceum's American owner, Colonel Bateman, Irving proved to be an electrifying actor. When only four years later, Bateman died, Irving took on the management of the theatre as well.

The next two decades saw the Lyceum become the cultural powerhouse of the capital and, thanks to it success, one of the most fashionable places to be seen as well. This was the result of Irving's combination of Victorian melodramas (most notably The Bells) in which he excelled, and a series of lavish Shakespearean productions in which he starred opposite Ellen Terry, one of the most beautiful, as well as gifted actresses of the century. Amazingly, she carried on acting into the era of the silent movies so one can see this star of the 1880s on film, with Ivor Novello and Gladys Cooper, in The Bohemian Girl (1922).

Irving's domination of London's theatreland was largely due to his talent on stage, his relationship with Ellen Terry and his ability to spot and employ young actors and actresses of promise, but it was also due to his inspired choice of business manager --- a stage-struck Irishman called Bram Stoker. Remembered these days for his novel Dracula (1897), Stoker was an indispensable help to Irving, and wrote a highly entertaining and informative book about his time with the great actor-manager.

Among many anecdotes was one describing a visit to the seaside, in search of peace and quiet. An old fisherman agreed to row them both out to sea for a couple of hours relaxation. As they set off, a crowd gathered on the shore, waving frantically. Irving, accustomed to the adulation of the public, waved regally and smiled, acknowledging their applause, while the fisherman carried on rowing out to sea, where a number of Royal Navy warships were to be seen in the distance. Suddenly there was a tremendous explosion as a sheet of water rushed towards the sky. "Oh Lord," said the fisherman, "I forgot. They're testing them new torpedoes today !" The crowds had not been cheering England's finest actor --- they had been desperately trying to warn him to get back to shore.

Irving's reign ended in 1902, partly due to old age, partly due to changing public taste, but largely because of the inevitable curse of theatreland --- fire. A huge fire destroyed his vast warehouse full of the scenery and costumes that he had accumulated over twenty years, and he could not afford to replace it all.

His leaving was rapidly followed by the demolition of the theatre (though the facade was retained). Shortly before the hallowed walls were pulled down, over a thousand actors gathered in the auditorium for a meeting at which it was decided to ask the government to support the creation of a National Theatre. A historic moment, even if it took many years finally to achieve.

The Lyceum's subsequent history was varied, to say the least. Reopened in 1904 as a music hall, in competition with Oswald Stoll's London Coliseum in St. Martin's Lane, the theatre changed hands again six years later, and was then the setting for variety shows, musicals and ballet, Ninette de Valois making her London debut there in 1915.

The Melville brothers, who had run the theatre since 1910, died within a year of each other, in 1937 and 1938, after which the Lyceum was closed as part of a road-widening scheme --- the theatre was to be replaced by a roundabout ! The last performance before the Lyceum was closed was of Hamlet, in which John Gielgud played the lead role. Another great Shakespearean actor, Donald Wolfit, attempted, after the War, to save it as a playhouse, but his gallant efforts failed, and it was converted into a dance hall, then was allowed to rot until Apollo Leisure refurbished and reopened it in 1996, with a production of Andrew Lloyd Webber's Jesus Christ, Superstar.

After leaving the Lyceum, walk back up Wellington Street, then turn left into Tavistock Street, which runs behind the Theatre Museum. This takes you into Southampton Street where, almost immediately opposite, stands David Garrick's house, an elegant eighteenth century mansion with a bronze-coloured plaque and bas-relief profile of the great actor, whose association with the theatre royal, Drury Lane has already been described.

Dr. Samuel Johnson, the compiler of the first English dictionary, was an admirer of Garrick, of whom he said, in a phrase that could as easily have been applied to Henry Irving a century later, "Here is a man who has advanced the dignity of his profession." His epitaph on hearing of Garrick's death, became famous, and has been applied to many other public figures. "I am disappointed in that death which has eclipsed the gaiety of nations and impoverished the public stock of harmless pleasure."

Having looked up at Garrick's house, carry on straight ahead into Maiden Lane.

Maiden Lane

An attractive old street, this is the site of Rules restaurant (see chapter on London's theatre restaurants) which has been a favourite with actors successful enough to afford the prices, since it first opened in the 1790s. It is the oldest restaurant in London. On the left are the stage door of the Vaudeville and Adelphi theatres. Today's Adelphi stage door is immediately next to what used to be the stage door --- the latter has a rather battered-looking Royal coat of arms over it. It was just outside the original stage door that William Terris, a handsome leading man who had learnt his trade under Henry Irving at the Lyceum, met his death ; a jealous fellow actor stabbed him to death. It is said that his ghost has been seen in the area.

At the end of Maiden Lane turn right into Bedford Street and head north, until you come to the junction with New Row, Garrick Street and King Street. On the left, some way into Garrick Street, can be seen the Garrick club, a gentlemen's club named after David Garrick. It has many actor members but no actresses, as women are allowed in only as guests. The recently cleaned exterior, a relic of Victorian London, hides a splendid interior and a remarkable collection of memorabilia.

The Garrick Club first opened in 1831 at 35 King Street, just nearby. Actors Charles Kemble and W.C. Macready were original members. Thackeray who was an early member became the best-loved of all. Today the Club is full of actors, writers and artists.

Turning right, one enters King Street, an attractive road of eighteenth century houses, smart coffee houses and cafes, and the site of, on the corner with Garrick Street, the world famous clothes shop, Moss Bros. Many an actor has made the pilgrimage to this stately building in order to be properly clothed (morning suit, with black morning coat and grey and black striped trousers, with black top hat) for an investiture at Buckingham Palace, to receive a decoration or, in a few cases, Knighthood or Damehood, for services to the theatre. This transformation is all the more marked these days, when actors and actresses, off stage, look no different to the rest of the public. A far cry from the 1940s and 1950s, when Binkie Beaumont, the doyen of London theatre managers, who dominated the commercial West end, insisted that his stars dress like stars !

St Paul's, Covent Garden

A low, narrow turning on the right of King Street, shortly before reaching the crowded Piazza, leads to the churchyard of St Paul's, an oasis of greenery and flowers in the heart of the city.

If anything, the main body of the church is even simpler than the facade. Although simplicity has its attractions, it can lack character, but St Paul's more than makes up for the lack of architectural detail by the profusion of plaques and commemorative tablets to generations of actors and actresses.

Most of the famous names of British film and theatre can be found here, in the Actors' church, which is frequently the setting for packed memorial services for the best known members of the profession. Noel Coward, Terence Rattigan, Ivor Novello, Vivien Leigh --- all are commemorated here. At the very back of the church the plaques are of wood, and there is a charming tradition of adding to the usual details of name and dates of birth and death, an appropriate quotation from a play (usually Shakespearean) to illustrate the character of the person. Vivien Leigh's, for example refers to death having in his possession "A Lass Unparalleled".

As in books, so on walls, it is often the things that are left out that tell us as much as those that are said. Jessie Matthews was a star in the 1930s. Her slim figure and huge eyes, together with a sweet singing voice and her talent as a dancer (the Americans had wanted her to appear in films with Fred Astaire) had made her the highest paid female performer in the country, both on stage and in a series of British films. Unfortunately she was as headstrong as some of the characters she played. One of her better songs, Gangway, summed up her approach to life, which included a ruthless disregard for other people's marriages.

Her seduction of Sonny Hale, the husband of the beautiful and very popular (within the profession as well as among the public) Evelyn Laye, was the last straw, and it was this action that is thought to be the reason that Jessie Matthews, despite her fame, has never had a plaque named after her in St Paul's. More appropriately, perhaps, she has had a bar named after her by one of her greatest fans, Andrew Lloyd Webber, in the nearby Adelphi theatre in the Strand.

It seems appropriate, given that Covent Garden originated with a church garden, that we should have ended the walk, as we began, at St Paul's Church, where Ellen Terry's ashes rest in a silver casket, and where generations of theatre cats are quietly buried in the bushes of the churchyard.

St Paul's Church. The Actor's Church

Wall plaques inside Church.

Postscript

Having lived in Covent Garden for over twenty years, I'm including a short history of how I got here as well as a description and photos of some of the most interesting places in the present day. As a student at the Guildhall School of Music and Drama, which in those days was down in Blackfriars near the Embankment, I lived in Bloomsbury in Southampton Row, walking down the Kingsway every day, along Fleet Street and down to John Carpenter Street in Blackfriars. Coming home late at night, I'd watch the great newspaper presses running in the back of these old buildings, and the newly printed papers coming out on conveyor belts, to be bundled and put into the waiting trucks lined up in the back streets. Next day's paper! It was thrilling and exciting to watch all the action. A lost world now as the presses have all moved out of town. It was years later before I moved to Covent Garden.

While I was studying at the Guildhall, I took a part time job, front of house, at the Old Vic Theatre. There, I met the actors and directors, and would hear of upcoming auditions but never had the chance to attend them. Then after leaving drama school, I became an assistant stage manager for the Felixstowe Repertory Theatre Company, a weekly Repertory Company as well as playing small parts. Each week I would dash down to London for auditions, and especially at the Old Vic. Finally it paid off and I was asked to join the company to tour Australia. The leads were to be Katharine Hepburn and Robert Helpmann, playing three plays in every capital city for six months.

On the ship coming back from Australia with the company, I met and subsequently married the ship's surgeon and moved to

Canada, and continued my acting career in Toronto. There was not much stage work there but some television. These were the days when TV dramas were shot live with no room for mistakes or retakes.

A few years later, we moved to Paris and I opened a small English speaking theatre, for theatre lovers who were having problems with the language. It was a challenging experience, especially raising a son there who ended up speaking French like a native. When not working, every weekend we would search out another famous chateau in the Ile de France or down on the Loire. But I still missed London.

.Years later returning to London, acting jobs were few and far between because I had been away for so long so I decided to start writing.

One morning, I went to visit the Theatre Museum, which was then on the corner of Bow and Great Russell Streets. It was a large collection with two main galleries, with very impressive exhibits. Viewing all the costumes, programmes, portraits, I wondered just how much personal sacrifice did these great actors experience, when working in the theatre. Surely all successful actors have experienced the anguish of often having to choose between their personal lives and their life in the theatre. After weeks of research I wrote a proposal to the Director of Events at the Museum and asked if it would be possible to present a script there called "Love From Shakespeare to Coward" based on this research. They said 'yes' and I presented it there, on and off for the next six years.

To promote the first month I invited Corin Redgrave and Dan Thorndike, nephew of Dame Sybil, to act together, so we had two members of two great theatrical families together on stage. A Redgrave and a Thorndike. Corin also invited his daughter, Jemma one Sunday, and we also had Laurence Olivier's daughter, Tamsin, on the same Sunday acting together, which is probably the only time they have done so.

We did the performances in the Picture Gallery, a large lovely room with red plush curtains, deep red carpeting and a collection of theatre portraits on the wall from the private collection of Somerset Maugham…brought from his villa in the south of France after his death. It was a wonderful atmosphere to work in as some original costumes worn by Ellen Terry, Sarah Siddons and Henry Irving just a few feet away in the next room.

It became my full time job. I wanted to help young drama students who had just left drama school to find jobs, Some of them couldn't even get auditions, no one would see them, they had trained for two or three years and couldn't find agents who would give them a job. You have to be extremely strong and use all your initiative to carry on during these desperate times. I put an ad in The Stage for actors who had some classical training, and received over 200 letters and photos in one week. I auditioned them, and tried to give them all some work inviting agents and managers to come to see them. It was one of the greatest pleasures helping young drama students get their first jobs, or first agents.

Most well known actors will tell you their awful stories of rejection, depression and hopelessness, before they got their big break. Others just give up and do something else entirely. Rejection is just part of the whole process of being an actor.

Every so often we would change the anthology and replace it with new material. One show was called 'A Tribute to Noel Coward' and everyone did something by Coward. It astonished me that some of the young actors who auditioned, had never heard of Coward. I asked one girl to go out and buy one of his recordings. The clerk at the shop was not helpful, asking 'what group does he play in?'

When the Museum was not available, we held these showcases as they had now become, not far away, at the home of The

Concert Artistes's Association at 20 Bedford Street. The Club rents out the main room, a small auditorium with stage and dressing rooms, when they are not using it themselves. Every Monday night they hold their own show, which consists of the members getting up and performing for their fellow members, also including members who have just joined and want to showcase their own material.

Some of the members including Pamela Cundell, Glenn Hayes, Jules Mannheim, Kenny Gibson, Ruth Allen and current President, Joan Savage are seasoned pros, and they keep the club alive with their wonderful anecdotes, when they are not off working in TV or a theatre somewhere. The Club bar upstairs, for members only, is a cheery place to have a drink and hear some of their stories. The CAA is a theatrical charity helping people in the profession who are in need. They have a retirement home for elderly performers called Brinsworth House located in Twickenham.

This is the area of London where the students of architecture, history, theatre, art, opera, ballet come here to learn, listen and experience once a life time performances that they will never forget. It is the most exciting theatrical district in London even before Irving and Bernhardt played here.

During these years I joined many theatre societies and went to their meetings, many of them held at the CAA. The First Nighters Club, was one of the best. The then President, the late Stephen Marshall, and a committee who chose a celebrity guest speaker each month ran it. Their old 'Year books' show many famous speakers from Noel Coward to Gillian Lynne. Up to the 1970's these first nighters would attend all the first nights in the West End, usually sitting in the Gallery or 'Gods' as they were called. They were severe critics but were often close followers of whoever was onstage that night. Now since the policy of having preview performances before an opening night, there are literally no more 'first nights' so the group was disbanded, much to the dismay of the members. Then there is the Ivor Novello

Society, the Henry Irving, the Max Wall, and meetings held at the private theatre Club, the Green Room Club. This Club was in underground rooms when it was in Adam Street, off The Strand, and at one very crowded meeting when Peter Ustinov was the speaker, it is said that he quipped, 'This is like giving a talk in a crowded submarine."

The Theatre Museum did not have a large budget to advertise or to promote the presentations. So I had to find an audience somehow for my first few shows at the Museum. I would hand deliver flyers to all these Societies, also placed them under car windscreen wipers, all around the streets of Covent Garden, then go to the lobbies of B&B's in Bloomsbury, front desks at hotels and many other places, a time consuming round each week..

One morning when delivering some flyers to the Green Room Club they told me that someone leaving the Club the night before, obviously drunk, had punched a hole, with a lit cigar, in their very large oil painting of Edmund Kean, which hung on the wall just inside the front door. The door was upstairs from the Club rooms, so no one could see who had done it. It was terrible vandalism and might cost a fortune to repair. I offered to do it with my oil paints and equipment as I had studied art in earlier days. So with some canvas, paint and care it took quite some time, but they seemed pleased with the result. The last time I saw the painting, it was re-hung out of harm's way, high up behind the bar. Since then the Club closed at that address and at the time of writing is now located in the Phoenix Arts Club, which is adjacent to the Phoenix Theatre.

I hope that they took Edmund Kean with them.

While presenting my show at the Museum during those years, I realized that some of the most recent graduates from drama schools hadn't really been told about the great actors and actresses who worked more recently than Sarah Siddons or Ellen Terry. There was a very large gap when even the artists of the last century were not included in their curriculum. People like Sybil

Thorndike, Lewis Casson, Fay Compton, Edith Evans, Alistair Sims Rachel Kempson, Diana Wynyard, Peggy Ashcroft, or even more recent ones such as Janet Suzman, Claire Bloom, and Dorothy Tutin, let alone the famous male actors. I decided to ask Rachel Kempson, (Lady Redgrave) to come out of retirement and take part in a reading of my latest play called 'Jamaica Interlude" I took her the script, and she agreed. The story of the play was very similar to real life. A group of actors decide to go on holiday to visit Noel Coward's old home, Blue Harbour in Jamaica, which is now a Bed and Breakfast place. Dramatic things happen there, before they all return to London. I wished that I could have invited Ian McKellan to play in it but he was in New York at the time.

I first met Ian McKellan, before he became a Knight, at a reception at the Theatre Museum, then again in New York when I wrote to congratulate him on the play he had just finished playing in, in London called 'Cowardice' written by Sean Mathias who also directed. I tried to interest two New York producers in the play, Sean and I discussed this possibility over lunch even though they had not read the play, and because of the small cast it could well interest them. As yet, it still hasn't happened. Janet Suzman played the lead opposite Ian and the dramatic climax of when she kills him at the end of the play is especially meaningful to an actress who is caught in an impossible personal dilemma.

During the following years, I found getting acting jobs few and far between so I started trying to write plays for all the actors who were in my shows. Three were eventually produced at the King Head Theatre in Islington, when Dan Crawford was still the owner.

Two more plays were done in New York shortly after, so I subsequently spent two years over there. While there I worked as Yul Brynner's personal assistant on his final tour of 'The King and I.' After he died, before returning to London I wrote to the Cunard Line to enquire if I might present my anthology on board the Q.E.2. They forwarded my request on to a lady who lived in Banbury, Diane Coles, who revolutionized the libraries on Cunard ships, and was in charge of lecturers and speakers on board. She was a visionary who was responsible for updating the old styled libraries with only volumes on Dickens and Twain, and perhaps a dictionary and a Bible. She went on to update many other cruise lines libraries. Diane then asked if I would like to help launch a "Literary Festival" for Cunard Lines which involved inviting best selling authors to sail on a trans-Atlantic crossing talking about their books. I joined the first crossing when we had invited George Plimpton to launch the Festival on board. It was a great success but Diane died tragically young, and we no longer ran the Festival. I returned to England. She is still missed by dozens of friends.

Back in Covent Garden, one unforgetable evening, I went to see a Charity show at the Theatre Royal in Drury Lane, produced by the impresario, Barry J Mishon, who specialized in presenting one-off Charity evenings. It was a presentation of Cole Porter's musical 'Nymph Errant' with stars such as Elizabeth Welsh and Alexis Smith. The evening was magical, with a full orchestra and chorus. The next day I wrote a letter to Barry whom I had never met, congratulating him on such a wonderful show, and saying that if he ever needed an assistant for his next show, I would love to work with him. I enclosed my resume and contact details.

A week later I received a phone call from him, he wanted to see me. He told me his assistant had left on a leave of absence and he needed someone, as he was planning his next show. It didn't take me long to find his office in Covent Garden, an old building, that used to be called the Potato building, the corner of Bow and Great Russell St. directly above the Theatre Museum! It was the building where all the potatoes were stored for the Market, in past times. It seemed such a coincidence that his office was just nearby the Drury Lane theatre.

His next show was to be a Gala Evening featuring the Leading Ladies of the Golden Age of Hollywood musicals! How he could imagine finding and bringing over from California, all those world famous stars to do a Charity performance in London, took my breath away. But he did it. Working in his tiny office, side by side, I answered the phone and sent faxes…this was before computers and e mails. When he was out of the office at lunchtime or at a meeting, when I answered the phone I never knew who would be at the other end of the line. Anything was possible. 'This is Claudette Colbert speaking" or another time, 'This is Nancy Reagan here"..Barry invited them all. The cast list started to grow. There were the obvious details to be done. Their air travel, first class of course, hotel suites, limousines to rehearsals and the show. Reception afterwards and press conferences. We had signed Ginger Rogers, Jane Powell, Alice Faye, Katherine Grayson, Arlene Dahl, to name just a few, as well as Van Johnson, just for starters. Michael Law and his Piccadilly Orchestra played at the Reception afterwards for dinner and dancing which was held in the Palm Court at the Waldorf Hotel. It was a magical evening. Barry went on to booking the artists for various nightclubs both in London and New York, concentrating at first on the Pizza-on-the-Park. His work has been an inspiration to other producers especially for one-off Charity Galas that are truly memorable.

I have written about the reading with Rachel Kempson but I had no idea that I would have the opportunity of going to see Blue Harbour myself. Rachel had been married to Sir Michael Redgrave and they were both very close friends of Noel Coward, so she must have been invited out there quite frequently. Several years later I did visit Blue Harbour and this time, instead of writing a play, I wrote a novel about the place, called Blue Harbour Revisited. The house has not been changed since Coward lived there. Some of his books, photographs and furniture are still there and I was given his old bedroom for my stay. His room is on the top floor, with a door leading out on to the balcony, which overlooks the sea and mountains beyond. It is a breathtaking view, and that night as a full moon came up, the sheer beauty of the place was very moving. The garden is below the house, and there are two small guest villas in there, with paths leading down to the swimming pool, and beach. All the stars used to come and stay when he lived there. From Katharine Hepburn, Marlene Dietrich, Alec Guinness, the Oliviers, Dame Joan Sutherland, Sean Connery, among many others. Finally he had to build himself a little one bedroom cottage up on the hill behind the house, so he could live there without the distractions of the main house and the guests.

At the time of writing, Blue Harbour is up for sale, but they are still in business as a B&B if anyone is interested in staying in such a beautiful spot with so many historical connections to the theatre, it is a great opportunity to see Coward's home.

It seems that all my work and opportunities have been in the area of Covent Garden. One of the happiest times, was when Late Joys, the name if the shows that The Players used to do, was when they were located in the Duchess Theatre in Covent Garden. They subsequently moved back to Villiers Street only to disband several years later. The last lines of one of their signature songs.

"Never mind the abuse, you have the excuse,

You went to Covent Garden in the morning."